HEADHUNTERS AND HOW TO USE THEM

OTHER ECONOMIST BOOKS

Guide to Analysing Companies
Guide to Business Modelling
Guide to Business Planning
Guide to Economic Indicators
Guide to the European Union
Guide to Financial Markets
Guide to Management Ideas
Numbers Guide
Style Guide

Dictionary of Business
Dictionary of Economics
International Dictionary of Finance

Brands and Branding
Business Consulting
Business Ethics
Business Strategy
China's Stockmarket
Dealing with Financial Risk
Economics
Globalisation
Successful Mergers
The City
Wall Street

Essential Director
Essential Economics
Essential Finance
Essential Internet
Essential Investment

Pocket Asia
Pocket Europe in Figures
Pocket World in Figures

HEADHUNTERS AND HOW TO USE THEM

A guide for organisations and individuals

Nancy Garrison Jenn

THE ECONOMIST IN ASSOCIATION WITH
PROFILE BOOKS LTD

Published by Profile Books Ltd
3A Exmouth House, Pine Street, London EC1R 0JH
www.profilebooks.com

Typeset in EcoType by MacGuru Ltd
info@macguru.org.uk

Printed in Great Britain by
Clays, Bungay, Suffolk

A CIP catalogue record for this book is available
from the British Library

ISBN 978 1 86197 734 2

The paper this book is printed on is certified by the © 1996 Forest Stewardship
Council A.C. (FSC). It is ancient-forest friendly. The printer holds FSC chain of custody
SGS-COC-2061

FSC
Mixed Sources
Product group from well-managed
forests and other controlled sources

Cert no. SGS-COC-2061
www.fsc.org
© 1996 Forest Stewardship Council

Contents

Acknowledgements

Many thanks to all those who helped me in my research for this book, in particular John Barker (UK Cabinet Office), Rudy Baert (Danone), Bruce Beringer (33 St James's), Virginia Bottomley (Odgers Ray & Berndtson), Jenny Bryant (Vodaphone), Luiz Cabrera (Amrop Hever), Ben Cannon (Heidrick & Struggles), Christopher Clarke (Boyden), Luis Conde (Amrop Hever), Tim Cook (Egon Zehnder), Peter Duffy (BG), Peter Felix (Association of Executive Search Consultants), Anthony Harling (Eric Salmon), Simon Hearn (Russell Reynolds), Rudy Kindts (BAT), Russell King (Anglo American), Mark Linaugh (Ogilvy & Mather International/WPP), David Lord (Executive Search Information Services), Nicholas Mabin (Cap Gemini, Ernst & Young), Manuel Marquez (Spencer Stuart), Robin Roberts (Egon Zehnder), Carol Scambler (State Street Bank), Steve Smith (Odessa), Charles Tseng (Korn/Ferry), Chris Van Someren (Korn/Ferry), Matthew Wright (Russell Reynolds), Fergus Wilson (Spencer Stuart) and Peter Wright (Estée Lauder). Grateful thanks also to my editors, Virginia Thorp and Penny Williams.

Nancy Garrison Jenn
February 2005

1 The search business

Executive search consultants do not come cheap – the clue to their value is in the name. Headhunters do not add value administratively or in a mechanistic recruitment sense. They add value with knowledge of the market, creative suggestions or an alternative view of individuals who are demonstrably able to deliver the results you want, or they may be aware of suitable individuals who have legitimate reasons for moving to another employer. Headhunters are searching not sifting.

Steve Smith, business consultant, Odessa International,
and former director of European human resources, Franklin Templeton Investments

There are an estimated 5,000 firms worldwide claiming to do retained executive search, which means they are employed by a client to find a senior-level candidate with a compensation package usually above $150,000. Choosing the right firm is crucial, as is ensuring that you work effectively with your headhunter to produce the desired outcome.

This book is a guide to help individuals and companies decide how to go about choosing a headhunting firm that best suits their needs and how to use them to best advantage when they have chosen a firm or firms. It looks at the leading firms in executive search and provides helpful advice on maximising a relationship with a search firm for both individual candidates and corporate users. It provides practical tips for job seekers on networking with headhunters, as well as a strategic analysis of trends and issues in the executive search profession and how search firms are diversifying into related services. There are profiles of the 20 leading global firms and details of leading search consultants by sector and industry in these firms and in the best specialist boutiques.

Definitions

Headhunters earn a living by identifying the best candidates for a specific job vacancy. To be able to do this effectively, they must understand the sector or industry in which they work. They must also have a good network of contacts within the sector and a knowledge of individuals' motivations or career interests. Most consultants handle about 20 searches a year, but this number is highly variable and can be much lower if, for example, the consultant is involved in management appraisals or other services that headhunting firms are involved in.

Executive (or retained) search

Executive search is the term used when headhunters are hired to find senior executives, from senior functional or line managers to chief executives, typically at base salaries of $150,000 upwards. Firms conducting this type of search are typically divided into large global players and small specialists or "boutiques".

This type of search is often known as retained search because a fee or retainer is paid which is not usually refundable, even if the search is unsuccessful. A portion of the retainer is normally paid in advance. The minimum fee for most retained search firms is about $50,000, but fees are more commonly calculated as a percentage (perhaps 33%) of the candidate's annual salary. Expenses are also payable to cover travel, meeting costs and communications. Large firms also charge "allocated expenses", which are research, secretarial and technology costs and can be around 4–8% of the retainer. But everything is, of course, negotiable, as is made clear later in this chapter.

Contingency recruitment

Contingency recruitment is when a fee is paid only if the position is filled successfully. In general, contingency covers the $75,000–150,000 salary range but it is by no means exclusive and varies by country. This method is firmly established in the United States, where it represents almost half of the total recruitment market. Besides the difference in the way the fee is charged, contingency recruitment and executive search differ in the type of service provided. Retained fees are paid for the process of searching, whereas contingent fees motivate recruiters to promote attractive candidates to clients.

Advertised recruitment

For recruitment and selection at mid-management levels the primary vehicle is often media advertisement such as newspapers. Retained search firms will sometimes offer a "selection" service for middle-management posts at lower levels. The usual retained search fees apply. Firms operating on a contingency basis that offer an advertised service will be paid only if they fill the position, though advertising costs are borne by the client. In advertised recruitment the client's name may or may not be divulged. It is also used for unusual recruitment where candidates might not be identified easily and in some fields such as government or education, where vacancies must be announced.

Internet recruitment

This is recruitment by website, mostly at mid-management levels up to $120,000. It involves a reactive, or applications-based, approach and a fee is normally charged only for the posting of the advertisement and not for the placement. Sometimes the client's name is divulged, which can be a major attraction for candidates. The market leader is www.monster.com.

Headhunting: a chronological checklist

The relationship between a client company and a search firm begins with an initial conversation in which the client explains its manpower needs and the search firm explains why it is well suited for the assignment. Once contracted, or retained, by a company, a headhunter prepares a job specification, draws up a target list of candidates, interviews the client company and begins to approach candidates. Each headhunting assignment follows a similar pattern. The following represents what happens when the search is for a senior executive in a publicly listed company:

- Initial client meeting with key account manager and the executives that will make the decision on the client side.
- Proposal letter sent from the headhunter to the client and/or a letter of engagement sent by the client to the headhunter. In either case, the result is a detailed document which acts as a control on the search and outlines the expected time plan and the headhunter's fees
- Assignment and signed contract: the commission mandate from a client to a headhunter to carry out a search for a specific position.
- Brief profile sent to client: a detailed document which summarises the job opportunity and will be shown to prospective candidates.
- File run: research in search firm's internal database. This should be done at the beginning of the search, but sometimes search firms do it before they get the job to demonstrate knowledge of the sector.
- Outside research: additional research including cold calls to target firms, use of industry directories and calls to contacts in the same sector. Some researchers only do internal desk work, some call and approach candidates, and others even conduct interviews. It depends on the firm and the assignment.
- Review meeting: usually four weeks into the search the

headhunter reveals where they have looked and why, and which candidates have been found.

◼ Long list: the initial list of all possible candidates for an assignment. It is usually compiled by research before candidates are approached by the headhunter.

◼ Screening by headhunter: the process of working through a large number of preliminary candidates in order to arrive at a shortlist.

◼ Candidate interviews by headhunter and candidate appraisal.

◼ Benchmark candidates: evaluation of candidates according to set criteria, often an individual known to the client and headhunter.

◼ Shortlist: the final list of candidates presented by the consultant to the client, typically three or four possible contenders, all of whom have expressed real interest in the position.

◼ Client interviews with shortlisted candidates.

◼ Reference checks: the search consultant asks individuals who know or have worked with the candidate for a reference. Sometimes these are made for the shortlist, sometimes only for the final candidate and/or the second or "back-up" candidate.

◼ Negotiation, conclusion, placement, completion: successful assignment completed by the search firm. Candidate accepts the position. Completion may be when a candidate starts work, sometimes when they sign a contract of employment and sometimes when they resign from their current job.

◼ Follow-up: the headhunter follows the candidate for the first 100 days in his new position to make sure that the move is a success. After this, the headhunter may continue to stay in touch, but on a more casual basis.

In the case of a smaller company looking for a middle to senior manager, the process will be simpler and shorter.

Origins

Often the best solution to a management problem is the right person.

Edwin Booz, founder of Booz Allen Hamilton

The United States

The executive search business began in the United States in 1926 when Thorndike Deland launched a business that charged a $200 retainer to find expert buyers for New York department stores. However, it was not until after the second world war that executive search gathered speed as part of the rapidly growing management consultancy business. It soon became evident to search consultants at McKinsey and Booz Allen Hamilton that the service might best be provided as a separate business. There was an inherent conflict of interest between recommending management change and then offering, for a fee, to fill the positions created. Furthermore, as large management consultancies took on more and more firms as clients, so more and more firms became off-limits as headhunting grounds.

McKinsey left the search sector in 1951. H. Wardwell Howell, head of the McKinsey search practice at that time, left to found Ward Howell, which became one of the biggest global search firms (until 1998 when its American division was acquired and the rest of the company rebranded itself as Signium). Handy Associates also broke away from McKinsey. Booz Allen Hamilton, which maintained its search activities until the late 1970s, groomed many of today's top search consultants. Among firms launched by its former management consultants are Boyden (1946), Heidrick & Struggles (1953), Spencer Stuart (1956) and Amrop Hever (1967).

Just like the management consultancies, the large accounting firms also built search practices, but they too faced potential conflicts with their audit services and suffered from many firms becoming off-limits for headhunting. A number of today's search firms have their roots in accountancy: Lester Korn and Richard Ferry left what is now KPMG to set up Korn/Ferry, and Russell Reynolds came from Price Waterhouse (now merged with Coopers & Lybrand as PricewaterhouseCoopers). Although some of the accountancy firms continue to offer recruitment in offices outside the United States, none maintain an American search practice, and most do mainly middle-management recruitment work for existing clients. A.T. Kearney is now the only large management consultancy with a search practice.

Europe

Executive search in Europe began some 15–20 years later. The first American search firm to arrive was Spencer Stuart, which opened an office in London in 1961 and in Paris three years later. In the search business, it is often called the "Grandfather of Search" in Europe, since it played the same "training ground" role as McKinsey and Booz Allen in the United States. Egon Zehnder left Spencer Stuart to found the first purely European search firm in Zurich in 1964, adding offices in Brussels, Paris and London by the end of the decade. London was the starting point for many firms, which were attracted by the large number of American corporations with offices there. Boyden, Korn/Ferry, Russell Reynolds and Heidrick & Struggles had all established themselves in the UK market by the end of the 1960s, targeting the top end of the market.

The first indigenous British search firms set up shop in the 1970s: GKR, founded by David Kay, Roy Goddard and Fred Rogers; John Stork, which was later acquired by Korn/Ferry; and in 1976 Whitehead Mann, now the largest firm in the UK having acquired GKR and financial specialist Baines Gwinner.

Expansion in Europe soon followed as hundreds of solo ventures and small firms developed out of the larger practices or were launched by enterprising executives with a background in human resources or management consulting. The larger firms then spread to Asia and Latin America, in the tracks of their multinational clients. Then came eastern Europe, China, Russia, India and the Middle East – all potentially rich hunting grounds for headhunting firms to explore, as they have seen their clients move into these emerging markets.

What drives the search business?

Like many other service industries, the fortunes of headhunters are tied to the economy. In the early 2000s, independent research conducted by Friedman, Fleischer and Lowe, San Francisco, into the relationship between search firm income and the economy, found a 97% correlation between the health of the general economy and that of the search industry. However, there are other underlying factors in play besides economic cycles. During the recession of the early 2000s, global firms found that average fees per assignment increased even though the number of assignments decreased. Recruitment at the very top remained constant because many CEOs were blamed for the bad situation.

Tough new financial legislation has led to increased business for search firms in the fields of legal, tax, compliance and auditing specialists in the United States and is expected to increase business in Europe as well. The Sarbanes-Oxley Act, introduced in the United States in 2002 to enforce better corporate governance following the collapse of Enron and other scandals, radically changed financial reporting requirements for American corporations. Search firms found that this and new regulation in Europe (the Eighth Company Law Directive) led to a significant increase in demand for board directors, CFOs, legal compliance officers, accountants and internal auditors. Russell Reynolds's CFO practice group saw a significant increase in business partially based on the new legislative requirements.

In 2004 the Olympic Games and an American presidential election created a significant amount of media hiring for large corporations wishing to take advantage of global advertising opportunities. This led to increased business for the media/entertainment sector groups at search firms, especially in the United States.

The bubble

In 1999, at the height of the dotcom boom, the worldwide search market was worth between $8bn and $9bn, but by 2003 it had collapsed to around $5bn-6bn. As more and more senior executives were hired, fired or simply changed jobs, in the second half of the 1990s the search industry grew by 15-20% a year. According to Christopher Clarke, CEO of Boyden:

> The average CEO in the United States lasted under three years, creating search opportunities. In addition, salaries were driven higher by the dotcom boom and related bubbles in financial services, media and support industries. There was the creation of an unprecedented number of new companies founded, funded and taken public by venture capitalists. All of these new start-ups needed CEOs to manage their public offerings. The associated stockmarket bubble gave some of the larger search firms the opportunity to launch their own stock at bubble prices and on the record of their inflated recent performances. Some of the funds raised were spent on overpriced acquisitions, diversification, poorly thought out IT investments, and inflated sign-on bonuses for search consultants. In this frenzy, client service suffered, and some firms introduced parallel processing – offering the same candidate to multiple clients on the basis of who could hire fastest. Reference checking and other standards fell and internal training was neglected.

And there, from an insider, is the reason the executive search industry found itself in deep trouble.

The shake-out

Things unravelled fast in early 2000 when the dotcom bubble burst and the stockmarket plummeted. Many firms laid off staff and were not looking to search firms for new people. This was made worse by Enron and other scandals, which hit investor confidence in the United States and other countries. The recruitment market dried up and slimmed down human resources departments tried to find candidates themselves to save money (and their own jobs). Procurement (purchasing) directors negotiated contracts with search firms, taking over this role from the HR director to cut costs drastically, making search more of a commodity business. A bloated search industry now found itself with substantial overcapacity and little work. There were mass layoffs by the larger firms. Korn/Ferry and Heidrick & Struggles, the biggest global players, each laid off over 700 people worldwide. Some firms resorted to radical price-cutting in order to keep old business and attract new clients, offering discounts and also extending the circumstances in which they would operate on a contingency-fee basis.

A number of overhead-heavy medium-sized firms found it difficult to compete against the powerful brand names of the global firms. Among those that cut back their operations fairly drastically were Ward Howell (now Signium), Norman Broadbent (especially in the United States), TMP (which sold its search practice, Hudson Highland) and Ray & Berndtson (the US business was acquired by A.T. Kearney). Many of the global firms slashed their international networks, especially in Asia, Latin America and eastern Europe, as multinationals reduced foreign investment to these markets and search opportunities dwindled.

Reshaping of the industry

As a result of the plight it found itself in, the search industry was forced to take a long, hard look at itself in the early 2000s. During this time some of the leading firms, including A.T. Kearney, Heidrick & Struggles, Hudson Highland, Korn/Ferry, Spencer Stuart and Whitehead Mann, changed their CEOs and other senior managers. Significant reorganisation and restructuring took place. For example, Korn/Ferry's internet recruitment venture, Futurestep, originally a one-service advertised selection/recruitment vehicle, was redesigned as a multiservice operation offering middle-management recruitment, project recruitment (when a client needs to hire a significant number of staff) and managed services (HR outsourcing).

Loss-making firms restructured their finances and developed a broader portfolio of services (board practices, executive coaching, management assessment and other consultative services) to help boost income.

The industry also started to become more professional. There was a new focus on ethics, reference checking, strict off-limits restrictions and quality of service. As John Grumbar, CEO of Egon Zehnder, notes:

> When times are tough, business is more difficult and the
> search industry tends to become more professional – when
> times are easy, standards tend to slip as it is easy to secure new
> business.

David Lord, an industry observer, feels that professional standards are improving only at the rate that clients become savvy enough to insist that standards be maintained or raised. He says:

> Violation of off-limits agreements and gaps in referencing and
> background checking are probably the most prevalent
> examples of unprofessionalism.

Recovery

Despite mixed economic signals, including a war in Iraq, an American election and fears about terrorism, which can make firms hesitant about hiring and investment, 2003 brought the first glimmer of hope for the search industry. Firms saw their first revenue growth since 2000 and with this a sense that the market for executive talent had improved, even if only modestly. Search firm chiefs were upbeat and attributed the recovery to the strength in corporate profits and general economic expansion. In 2003, Spencer Stuart saw a 14% upturn in revenues, Amrop Hever 10% and others experienced more modest growth. According to the *Executive Recruiter News* annual ranking survey of the 20 largest retained search firms worldwide and the 40 largest American retained firms for 2003, roughly half measured annual revenue growth in positive terms. The previous year only 25% of the firms reported any growth. As a whole, the 20 largest global firms registered a 2% increase in fee revenue in 2003, while the total for American firms showed no growth. Just a few years previously, the flat American figure would have been a great disappointment to a search market that had enjoyed such heady growth in the 1990s. Yet the 2003 figures indicated that the American search market had stabilised after three years of decline.

Matthew Wright, president Europe at Russell Reynolds, says:

> In 2000 we had the internet boom and the search market was

9

*robust with lots of new players. In 2002/03 we saw a market
downturn with too many players in the search profession.
Thus in 2004 we saw a consolidation with many of the
medium-sized search firms either leaving the business, being
acquired and/or moving downmarket. The search market is
more competitive now with clients more demanding, fewer
jobs, the selection of search firms in the hands of the
procurement (or purchasing) officer who typically attempts to
get prices down. Also we see the development of in-house
recruiting. HR directors want quality, speed and more value-
added thus there is an increased demand for ongoing market
intelligence, benchmarking, and in general, a more consultative
approach.*

Outlook

The signs of recovery in 2004 are being carried through into 2005, with
some firms seeing a return to growth rates reminiscent of the boom in
the late 1990s. Where is the growth coming from? Chris van Someren,
president, Korn/Ferry Europe, sees a resurgence in financial services
(investment banking, fixed income, asset management) and technology
(software and peripherals). Bruce Beringer, chairman, 33 St James's, adds
that there is increased demand for asset management, insurance, private
equity and compliance/regulatory specialists as a result of New York
attorney general Eliot Spitzer's aggressive pursuit of many American corporations. A 2004 ruling by America's Securities and Exchange Commission (SEC) states that 75% of all fund management boards must be
independent/non-executive. This meant that over 4,000 firms in the
United States needed to hire compliance officers or regulatory specialists during 2004–05, enlisting the aid of headhunters in the process. The
US Data Protection Act also implies that there will be much tighter regulation in all industries. This will lead to increased business for search
firms, particularly in the areas of compliance or regulatory specialists
and in the non-executive field.

There are conflicting opinions about whether the indicators bode
well or not for headhunters. The baby-boom generation is entering
retirement and the talent shortage is expected to intensify over the next
ten years. As a result some headhunters forecast increased business.
Paul Reilly, CEO of Korn/Ferry, says:

There is always a shortage of good talent and a demand for

good people. The retiring baby boomers will mean increased
business for the search profession.

However, Lord is not so certain. He confirms that companies by now are at least aware of the demographics and some are emphasising benchbuilding in anticipation of a tightening market. Benchbuilding is the recruitment or promotion of people to fill gaps in the management team usually identified as a result of a succession planning exercise. Many companies are already reporting that some searches are getting tougher. However, he says:

> *In my view this is a Y2K kind of issue: the problem (declining*
> *population in the heart of the labour market) is real but I don't*
> *think it will become a crisis, as some predict. Rather, I see*
> *retirement patterns changing (older people staying in the*
> *workforce on a project, part-time or freelance basis);*
> *continuing advancement of productivity; education; training;*
> *and higher pay in areas of exceptional shortages, all of which*
> *would ameliorate that situation.*

Trends in executive search

Consolidation of the headhunting industry has mirrored other service professions which have tended to evolve into global players and specialist, niche firms, often referred to as boutiques. There has been a tendency for multinational companies to consolidate their service providers. Many companies have one legal firm, one advertising agency and only one of the big audit firms to represent them worldwide, and now, increasingly, they are relying on one search firm.

The headhunting business is dividing into two main segments:

- large global firms such as Heidrick & Struggles, Korn/Ferry and Spencer Stuart, with offices worldwide, well-known brand names and global recognition;
- small specialised boutique firms, which tend to be concentrated in fewer sectors or industries and typically in one geographic market. For example, based in Europe, Rose Partnership and Blackwood Group specialise in financial services, Bird & Co in media and Zygos in board/non-executive directors. In the United States, Herbert Mines specialises in luxury goods and retail, and Gould McCoy Chadick Ellig specialises in consumer and industry.

In Asia, Eban, Global Sage and Executive Access specialise in financial services, and Bó Lè (now part of Stanton Chase) specialises in consumer.

Well positioned or out

The price of entry into the headhunting business to service a global company is high and to survive today a search firm has to be well positioned in its search offering and/or it needs to diversify into an expanded portfolio of services. For the top global firms brand image is crucial, and further development of their brand name is occurring in different ways (see Public versus private ownership opposite). Many of the medium-sized firms with revenues of between $10m and $50m were hit hard by the recession of the early 2000s. These firms found it hard to compete without a compelling point of difference from the global firms or the boutiques. In the American market, many small to medium-sized search firms are either being acquired or are being driven to work on a contingency basis (where they only bill the client if the search is completed).

Bob Damon, president, Korn/Ferry United States, says:

> There is no room left for the medium-sized firms. Medium-sized firms don't have the clout or global resources of the large firms or the economic structure of the small boutiques that can dedicate their resources to 1–2 sectors or industries and be entirely client-focused.

Re-emergence of boutique firms

Many individuals who set up small firms that were acquired in the boom and bust years have become independent again. Charles Polachi, a technology specialist, sold his firm Fenwick Partners to Heidrick & Struggles in 1998, assumed a management role at the firm in the technology field, then became independent again in 2002 when he started a new niche firm in technology, Polachi & Company (now part of ITP Partners). Kevin Conley, who specialises in financial services, sold his boutique firm Westgate Partners to Korn/Ferry in 2000, only to lose his job in 2001. He subsequently formed a new boutique called Conley & Co in 2002.

Small firms are often created when experienced consultants at larger firms tire of the bureaucracy and off-limits requirements and crave their independence. According to Beringer (founder of 33 St James's):

> *There is constant billings pressure in a global firm – you must*
> *do at least 12 searches a year minimum, and often, when you*
> *actually win an assignment, it is given to a researcher to do.*
> *With a boutique firm, what you see is what you get.*

The way Beringer sees it, a consultant in a boutique firm "lives, eats, sleeps and breathes the client, to whom he has complete dedication". Moreover, the consultant who signs the deal with the client is the one who does the work. This is not always the case in a global firm where assignments may be passed to a junior consultant whom the client has not met. However, the global firms are well aware of the passion and commitment of the boutiques and are developing key account managers to help a consultant team focus effectively on one client. At firms such as Korn/Ferry and Heidrick & Struggles, the objective of developing key client accounts is to do twice the business with half as many clients and to deepen and expand the relationship with the client.

Public versus private ownership

Among the global firms there is evidence of further subdivision between those that are stockmarket listed and those that remain privately controlled. Large public firms such as Korn/Ferry and Heidrick & Struggles, which must pay close attention to their stockmarket performance, are repositioning and expanding their offerings to include a more diverse portfolio of services such as management assessment and executive coaching (see below). In contrast, private firms such as Spencer Stuart, Russell Reynolds and Egon Zehnder are staying focused primarily on executive search and their partnership culture. Manuel Marquez, president, Spencer Stuart Europe, believes that being privately controlled has enabled the firm to benefit from maintaining a focus on the long term:

> *Concentrating on our core business, instead of seeking volume*
> *by expanding the portfolio of our services, seems to have paid*
> *us well.*

Korn/Ferry, however, clearly feels that its global clients want a seamless product offering in many areas of people management.
Paul Reilly explains:

> *In the early years of search, the pioneers, Richard Ferry and*

Russell Reynolds, established an industry by focusing on one area – executive recruitment. As all things evolve, now their firms are becoming providers of broader human capital solutions. All service professions have undergone this transformation into full-service providers (just look at the banks). Search is a younger industry than investment banking, advertising, law, consulting and so on; the same diversification and consolidation will happen here as it has in every other service segment.

Other leading global firms are positioned somewhere in between. For example, privately controlled firms Egon Zehnder and Russell Reynolds both offer search with an appraisal practice which is growing, and stockmarket listed firms Heidrick & Struggles and Whitehead Mann offer search, assessment and coaching.

Diversification into new services

Just like other professional services, search firms are now offering a broader range of services. For example, a typical financial services institution will have departments dealing with investment banking, consumer and retail banking, commercial and merchant banking, insurance, real estate and trading, bonds and wealth management. All these services used to be offered in separate companies. Jocelyn Dehnert, vice-chair, Heidrick & Struggles, London, sees the repositioning of the publicly listed search firms to offer a wider range of services as inevitable: "Clients find themselves under more public scrutiny and turn to the search consultants as trusted advisers." In her experience, clients need to know whether:

- they have the right team in place;
- team members are compensated correctly;
- succession plans are in place;
- they understand where competitive threats will come from.

Heidrick has set up a business unit for what it calls "leadership services", which includes management assessment, benchmarking of staff capabilities and comparing them with competitors, training and career coaching. Management assessment now accounts for 15% of the firm's revenue in southern Europe. Van Someren agrees that an integrated offering of services is the firm's main attraction to clients, especially those seeking to recruit managers for senior down to line manager posts, and to assess existing talent and attract new talent. For example, Korn/Ferry offers executive search, outsourced recruitment and management assessment.

Management assessment is usually done by the same consultants who conduct executive search. Coaching, however, is usually carried out by a separate division or team of consultants. For example, Whitehead Mann's The Change Partnership is a separate division, founded and led by Peter Hogarth, which offers coaching and leadership development and has been successful in developing a strong brand.

Diversification can also be seen as a response to changing demographics, as Reilly explains:

> With the baby boomer population ageing and retirement rates about to explode, today's leading companies are putting additional emphasis on their executive talent. Issues such as succession planning, retention and executive job satisfaction have become critical to HR professionals.

Do companies really want the diversified services that the search firms are offering? Lord feels that companies need services like this but see no particular reason to obtain them from search firms:

> What the search firms are doing is something they thought up to improve revenues, not something clients demanded from them.

This is a view echoed by Peter Wright, head of HR at Estée Lauder Cosmetics in New York:

> Many of the global search firms were forced to diversify as a reaction to the downturn in the economy. They did bring global economies of scale to their organisations and have diversified as a desperate measure rather than a reaction to what clients really want. ("Oh no, the revenue is down – what else can we offer?"). Search firms say they are providing a unique new service of management assessment but it is 95% conventional interviewing. Search firms don't understand the other services and provide them in a mediocre fashion.

It is too early to say which strategy – search only or diversified product offering or something in between – will prevail.

Integrated firm versus network

Global search firms can be organised as wholly owned, highly integrated firms or networks of independent, locally owned firms. There is a debate about which ownership structure better serves clients. Egon Zehnder, Spencer Stuart and Russell Reynolds are examples of integrated firms with one brand name, consistent standards and product offerings, and typically closer relationships between consultants worldwide with less argument about fees among countries. In contrast, Amrop Hever, IIC and Ray & Berndtson are examples of networks of locally owned firms which are less centralised and highly entrepreneurial. However, networks may provide inconsistent quality from country to country.

Integrated firms claim to be more tightly run and have consistent standards for quality, a one-brand image (which is important for attracting global clients and preferred-provider contracts) and more fluid cross-border, multicountry searches. By contrast, independent networks claim they are more entrepreneurial, more creative and have reorganised to better suit client needs. Under the leadership of Jim Conroy, IIC grew significantly during the difficult years of 2001–04 by identifying additional member search firms that would fit their culture and strengthen their industry focus (energy, financial services, automotive and manufacturing). Another network, Stanton Chase, also substantially increased its global footprint by adding 16 offices when it added Bó Lè in Asia and Ward Howell Euroselect in Vienna to its network.

However, can a network compete effectively with integrated firms for global business? According to Lord, to be successful with a major multinational client, a search network must:

- give an account manager the authority to make things happen in a network environment;
- demonstrate consistency of processes and procedures worldwide;
- possess a brand that will attract a talented candidate pool.

Thus to build a global business and a global brand, members of a search network must take their own local name off the door and be willing to adopt a common way of conducting searches and interacting with clients. This is not an easy proposition, although some firms, such as

Transearch, have been successful in doing this. Many local firms that make up a network have spent years developing their brand names and feel they will lose their identity. Also many local firms within the networks provide different services for their clients. This is a difficult issue that may take a long time to resolve.

Industry specialists

The days of the generalist are over. Recruiters have to compete intellectually and have the same market knowledge and expertise as their clients; they must be equals. According to Matthew Wright, a client will say "tell me something I don't know". Thus there is an increasing client demand for market knowledge and top-quality service from the consultant. "The client wants someone who gives them comfort as well as excitement," confirms Virginia Bottomley, a partner at Odgers Ray & Berndtson. "Excitement in this case translates into market knowledge and sensitivity so profound that it wows the client."

Functional specialists

Many search firms now have functional specialist practice groups to find and place chief financial officers (CFOs), chief information officers (CIOs), legal or human resources (HR) directors or IT managers, and have search consultants dedicated to functional specialties across industry sectors. For example, Russell Reynolds has a dedicated functional practice group called the "Corporate Officers" sector. Wright explains:

> The executive suite has become more visible, more scrutinised, more diverse and more important than ever before. Not that long ago, CFOs were smart accountants, general counsels were genteel attorneys, and HR (or personnel) directors were just nice. No longer. Today's CXOs must not only have solid grounding in the specific function, they must also be strategic thinkers, mentors, change agents, innovators and thought leaders. Because of this, it is now the case that many functional specialists in headhunting firms have worked in several industry and/or geographic sectors.

Individual stars give way to the team-driven approach

In the past, companies typically selected a search firm because of a star consultant who was highly visible. Many individuals in the search business have star quality and magnetism, such as Tom Neff (Spencer

Stuart) and Gerry Roche (Heidrick & Struggles) in the United States, and Anna Mann (formerly of Whitehead Mann), David Kimbell (Spencer Stuart) and Egon Zehnder (Egon Zehnder) in Europe. Having access to a well-respected consultant with a good network was the main reason a client was attracted to and stayed loyal to a particular firm. Star quality is less important these days. The stars, of course, are still around and are still important, but now search firms are driven much more by their industry practice groups, and the goal is cross-border teamwork across sector, function, industry and geographic market. In-depth market knowledge of a sector or industry afforded by the practice groups allows global firms to compete more effectively with boutiques. In effect, industry practice groups represent dedicated boutiques within global firms.

Stephen Lawrence, former CEO of Whitehead Mann, confirms that companies want a team approach with a key account manager who is clearly responsible. Interdisciplinary teams with different skill sets to solve a specific need are also becoming more common. According to Dehnert, a typical team might include a financial services specialist, a benchmarking specialist and a leadership services consultant. Clients require local market knowledge (for example, cultural sensitivity and local compensation levels) along with real functional depth and expertise (for example, a CFO specialist).

Although teams are increasingly important, this is, after all, a personal business where access to individuals is best provided by someone who is well respected, has credibility and knows the industry and corporate culture. Senior executives are more likely to reveal their personal ambitions to someone at their own level, with the qualities of a father confessor, than to a junior team member.

Global or regional emphasis

The days of dividing up European search into sub-regions such as southern Europe, northern Europe or Scandinavia are over, according to Manuel Marquez. There is an increasing emphasis on sector practice groups on a global or regional basis, and less on clustering of offices by sub-region or country. Within southern Europe, for example, Spain, Portugal and Italy have little in common. What makes most sense is to have local teams as well as regional and global teams. Spencer Stuart's global and European practice groups allow its consultants to work across borders. Other search firms are also organised this way. As if to reinforce this global or regional focus, search firms are moving from decentralised profit centres to global compensation models. Russell Reynolds, Egon Zehnder, Spencer Stuart and others have recognised that a regional or global compensation model removes some of the barriers to effective cross-border search. Egon Zehnder has a "one world, one firm" model which compensates all consultants based upon the firm's (and not the individual's) profits. This means that consultants are just as motivated to assist a partner in another market on a multicountry search as to conduct one in their own local market. Some firms have local compensation systems which can hinder cross-border work and do not encourage consultants to work outside their local area.

Preferred-provider approach

In the past, companies often retained several search firms at the same time. Investment banks were particularly prone to this approach because search was often decentralised and there could be 20–30 search firms working for the same bank with minimal co-ordination. Managing the relationships became cumbersome and costly. However, the downturn in the early 2000s and the need to cut costs led to fewer search firms being retained per firm. This led to companies developing preferred-provider agreements which had the effect of reducing the number of search firms and involved more functional control over searches being conducted. Such agreements are being used more and more and in most cases they work well. However, they have their limitations, as Anthony Harling, a consultant at Eric Salmon & Partners, London, explains,

> Once a company is tied into working with a specific firm (or a small number of firms) it can be limiting. We are in the people business and this kind of global agreement doesn't actually guarantee that you have the best individual search consultant to work with in each country. The individual consultant doing the search is still more important than the overall network or the brand name.

BG Group, an energy company based in the UK, has an unusual approach: it has designated six executive search firms as preferred providers and they must work together. Called The Resource Alliance, the group includes three global firms, two boutiques and one mid-market firm which meet on a regular basis. An advantage of this approach is that consultants are treated as part of the client's management team and they can anticipate recruitment needs in advance and not just the week before a departure or promotion. This type of approach may become more common in the future.

Balancing speed of delivery and quality of candidates

Finding a match between the ideal candidate and the cultural fit of the company has become increasingly recognised as important. Speed is still of the essence, too. However, even though clients are usually keen in theory to find and appoint someone as soon as possible and are presented with a shortlist to enable them to do that, in practice clients are taking longer to make a decision on who to appoint. And they may be right to do so in order to take the best long-term view. As Walter Williams of Battalia Winston, Boston, says:

> The client will remember the candidates who stayed ten years with the firm [and were successful in their roles], even if it took the recruiter longer to deliver them.

Headhunters justify the time they take on the grounds that they need to assess candidates rigorously according to core competencies and emotional intelligence, and that these competencies change from assignment to assignment. Search firms can suffer embarrassment when a high-profile appointment turns sour, as in the case of Anna Mann's role in the choice of Sir Ian Prosser as chairman-elect of J. Sainsbury, a UK supermarket group. (Sir Ian later withdrew after opposition from institutional shareholders.)

Fierce fee-cutting

Fees are typically paid as a percentage of the total compensation of the candidate or a fixed fee based on the complexity of the search. Many companies have sought to reduce the amount they spend on search fees. One of the ways to cut prices is to bundle search assignments and ask for a volume discount, for example five searches for a reduction in fees of 25%. Another way is for the client to offer the potential of further work. Alternatively, fees may be capped where the maximum amount to be paid has an upper limit. Fees can be fully retained: for example, one-third payable at the beginning of the assignment, one-third payable after 30 days and the final third payable after 60 days or assignment completion. Or they may be part paid as an initial retainer, part paid at the shortlist stage and part paid on completion.

According to Harling, fees are negotiable and are coming under increasing scrutiny. Many companies have transferred responsibility for fee negotiation from the HR department to the procurement department. Serious attempts at fee-cutting started in the early 2000s, the worst years for search, and have continued ever since. Once a search firm has offered to cut its fees or provide volume discounts, it is difficult to increase them again.

As the economy improves, there is likely to be less fee-cutting by the global firms as clients become less pressured to cut costs, particularly at the more senior levels. However, some consider that pricing in the search profession may evolve into the model used by law firms whereby the senior partners charge higher fees than the more junior ones.

The internet

Identifying potential candidates for jobs has become easier as there is so much information available on the internet. This makes the real challenges the depth of the appraisal or assessment, persuading people to move jobs and closing the deal. Roche offers these words of wisdom:

> Search is not identifying the tall ships on the horizon, but bringing them back and tying them up on the dock.

The internet can be an efficient vehicle for finding junior and mid-level candidates in the $80,000–120,000 salary range. Monster, Yahoo! Hotjobs, Harvey Nash and other targeted websites continue to thrive at these levels. There is also a growing number of specialist websites that efficiently target niche markets such as engineering, marketing, legal and media. However, the internet has had less impact on senior-level appointments, where executive search remains the preferred way to find first-rate candidates, particularly at salaries above $150,000. Nonetheless, the internet has enabled many small firms to develop effective global databases that may be a threat to the larger firms.

Paul Turner, a partner at Whitehead Mann, London, warns:

> Internet advances mean that all search firms, regardless of size, now have the ability to develop a cost-effective database. In some respects, search is becoming a commodity, and the firms must add value and develop a point of difference to retain

client loyalty. Search firms must differentiate themselves beyond their database. Recognising the need to add value we have developed the concept of leadership consulting and are focusing on its diversification efforts in the assessment and coaching/development fields.

In-house recruiting

Increased availability of information on executive-level candidates via the internet has motivated many companies to build internal teams to recruit directly at that level. In its 2004 Inhouse Recruiting Team Survey of Human Resource Professionals, Jones-Parker/Starr, consultants to HR and executive search consulting firms, found that almost 60% of 163 human resource executives at American corporations reported that they had or were considering the development of an in-house executive recruiting team. The trend was especially evident in financial services and technology, where a growing number of firms do more direct recruiting at executive level and use search firms more selectively. In some cases, these companies have reduced their use of search firms to 20% or less in searches to fill positions in the $150,000–300,000 range. Examples of this trend can be found at Abbott Labs, Cisco Systems, Dell, First Data Corp, J.P. Morgan Chase, Microsoft, Unisys, Wachovia, Washington Mutual and Wells Fargo.

In many cases, former retained search consultants are organising these initiatives and finding that direct approaches to senior-level candidates are more acceptable in the market and can help an organisation build a better understanding of the executive talent market as it applies to their needs. However, not all search consultants agree. Grumbar feels that in-house recruitment has several disadvantages:

- It is much harder to approach outside candidates especially from a competitive firm.
- Recruiters may lose touch with the marketplace and get bored during downtimes when there is not much in-house recruitment.
- In-house recruitment is not effective at board level: "You cannot ask an in-house recruitment consultant to find the CEO."

Currently in-house initiatives are mostly limited to the US, but some firms are exploring the model on a global basis, and European corporations are taking note of this trend. "This development by no means spells the demise of the executive search industry," says David Lord, an industry expert. "Rather it's a recognition of demographic forces that will drive an unprecedented need for search services during the next decade or so, and the realisation that all available mechanisms for identifying and recruiting leaders will be needed to compete effectively."

REGULATING THE HEADHUNTERS

The only form of accreditation that exists within the search industry is membership of the Association of Executive Search Consultants (AESC). Set up in 1959, the AESC has taken on the role of self-regulator. To become a member, firms must undergo reference checking (from clients and other search firms), a site visit and a vote by the appropriate AESC regional council. Each member must follow the association's code of conduct, which covers ethics and guidelines on professional practice. The AESC also helps people outside the industry understand what to expect through its "Bill of rights" for clients and candidates, and acts as a channel for complaints about search firms. (See Appendix 2 for a list of members.)

Peter Felix, president of the AESC, is well placed to comment on the ups and downs of the search industry, and below are his views on the current state of search and what lies ahead in terms of regulatory issues.

Is the search business becoming more professional?

There is greater pressure on search consultants to perform and to deliver competitive earnings. Clients have also become more demanding. These pressures do not always pull in the same direction and it can be tempting for consultants to cut corners to win business or to execute assignments. This is recognised as a poor long-term strategy, but some firms may be tempted to try the following:

- "Rusing" to obtain information under false pretences. For example, a firm pretends to be doing a search assignment but is actually seeking to source or identify individuals.
- "Floating" CVs on a contingent basis. For example, a consultant peddles CVs to a potential client without a specific mandate to conduct a search. This practice is more common in the United States where there are more contingency firms.
- Talking about candidates without their permission.

Although these examples do not breach government regulations, they do breach the AESC's Professional Practice guidelines and Code of Ethics, and increasingly laws such as those on data privacy will bring pressure to bear.

Overall, I think that professionalism is improving because it has to, and consultants are more aware of the consequences if they behave badly or in an unprofessional way. Journalists who are ready to seek out a recruiting scandal mean it is difficult to hide from exposure if a serious issue arises which could involve misrepresentation or lack of due diligence. In the United States, a number of search consultants have been taken to court when a hire has gone bad or when a hiring organisation is angry because it has lost a key executive through executive search. I am glad to say that most of these cases have been based upon questionable grounds and either dismissed or settled out of court for small amounts.

How is the relationship between search firm and client changing?

As demand for search hit an all-time high in the late 1990s, so too did examples of complacency, arrogance and aggression in pricing among search firms. However, once the recession hit, search firms immediately experienced a push-back on pricing and on consulting terms. The purchasing department increasingly became the first line of control on the use and cost of search firms and HR departments even started referring to executive search as a commodity service to be priced accordingly. By the end of the recession, mutual dissatisfaction had reached a high level and there was little empathy or understanding on either side.

However, some HR executives understood that an unsatisfactory relationship with their search firm was counterproductive and that more effort was needed to invest in the longer-term development of working relationships and to involve search firms more strategically. Much to the surprise of search firms, they began talking along the lines that many search firms have always desired, saying: "Let's move away from a transaction mind-set to longer-term relationships." Many search firms and clients are wrestling with these issues. Both sides need to be more flexible and contribute more to their relationship. The clients need to move away from transaction/contingency thinking and to put a stop to the purchasing department being involved in decisions that it is not equipped to make. The search firms need to talk to their clients more strategically and use their most sophisticated skills in these discussions. Search firms should be talking about issues that are not seen to be directly self-serving, such as retention, which is a big issue for clients.

What effect have corporate scandals such as Enron had on headhunters?

The overall environment for professional services has been changing. The corporate governance crisis that followed the collapse of Enron has had an impact throughout the developed world. The destruction of Arthur Andersen, a major professional services firm, sent warning signals throughout the professional services industry. All sectors would in future be scrutinised and exposed not only to possible regulation but also to investigation for any hint of malpractice. For the executive search profession, so far the shock waves have been minor, although there are clear indications in the United States, by nature a litigious society, that dissatisfied clients may take action against search firms that they believe have misled them or caused them consequential damage though unsatisfactory hires. In Europe, the traditionally secretive and clandestine profession has been dragged out of the closet and subjected to the harsh spotlight of media investigation and comment on issues such as board and executive appointments that have gone sour. Added to this has been the entry into the arena of search firms that became publicly quoted companies in the late 1990s. Followed by analysts and commented upon in the financial press, the conduct of these firms and their performance has become of critical importance to the search industry.

Are headhunters subject to governmental regulation?

Overall, the search profession is still largely unregulated by specific legislation. However, some regulation has already resulted from the corporate governance scandals, some of it ironically of benefit to the executive search profession because of the need for more careful selection and management of boards of directors. But other regulatory influences are at work that can and will affect the search profession. Data privacy legislation is spreading rapidly around the world and already affects most of the major economies. Europe, Canada, Australia and Japan have already enacted rigorous laws that directly affect the way in which executive search firms acquire and retain confidential information about candidates.

Since the EU introduced its data privacy regulations, the AESC has been negotiating with the working party concerned to develop a Code of Conduct on Data Privacy that specifically relates to retained executive search work. If agreement is reached, such a code of conduct would bind all members of the AESC in Europe.

Regional trends

Despite globalisation and the spread of business into new markets, North America still accounts for around 50% of the total revenue of executive search firms, and Europe for 35%. Asia, Latin America and Africa make up the remaining 15%. However, emerging markets such as China, India and Russia promise big opportunities for long-term growth.

North America

The executive search market in the United States is the largest and most developed in the world. There are over 5,000 search firms, many of which do middle-management recruitment and contingency search as well as retained executive search. Many trends began in the United

States, such as in-house recruitment and preferred-provider agreements. Speciality practice groups in the global firms also started there, and there is a high degree of specialisation that has not yet spread outside the country. Historically dominated by financial services and technology, American search firms have steadily diversified and developed expertise in a wide range of industry sectors. A look at some of the leading global firms reveals the diversity of sector, industry and functional expertise. There are dedicated specialists in biotechnology, medical devices, not-for-profit, media and entertainment, travel and hospitality, communications, software and emerging technologies. The list goes on and on, and continues to grow.

Recent market demand and the impact of the Sarbanes-Oxley regulations, as well as continuing SEC investigations into financial services, have created new requirements for managers and boards. Corporations are turning to search firms to help them assess the composition of their boards, the functional expertise of critically important roles such as the CFO, and risk management and compliance.

Europe

The UK has the largest and most sophisticated search market in Europe, second only to the United States in size. According to the AESC, around one-third of all executive searches in Europe are conducted in the UK. Its strength comes not just from financial services but also from the consumer and retail sector as well as biotechnology and life sciences. For many large search firms, the UK represents half of the financial services market in Europe. At Russell Reynolds, the UK accounts for 50% of the financial services practice in Europe, followed by Germany at around 18% and France at 11%. The firm sees Germany as an important area for expansion in financial services and is broadening its operations to include insurance, real estate and other related sectors.

After the UK, Germany and France are the next largest search markets in Europe. Although headhunters view the UK as the driver of search business within Europe, Germany is considered one of the principal drivers of the technology sector. Kai Hammerich of Russell Reynolds explains:

> The UK market is important because it is the bridgehead for American corporations in Europe with far more start-up investments than any other European country. However, Germany is the technology powerhouse of Europe because of

Table 1.1 **Executive recruitment firms in the UK by market share of net[a] fee income, 2004**

Rank	Firm	Market share of net fee income (%)
1	Whitehead Mann	7.6
2	Spencer Stuart	5.9
3	Russell Reynolds	5.1
4	Egon Zehnder	4.8
	Odgers Ray & Berndtson	4.8
6	Heidrick & Struggles	4.0
7	Korn/Ferry	3.6
8	Harvey Nash	2.7
9	Rose Partnership	1.7
10	Longbridge International	1.6
11	Hogarth Davies Lloyd	1.6
	Total	43.4

a Excluding reimbursed expenses.
Source: Executive Grapevine International Limited, *UK Directory of Executive Recruitment Consultants 2004-2005, Benchmark Survey: 184 Firms with more than 50% of assignments conducted above £100k*

> the sheer size of the market and also because of companies
> such as SAP, Siemens and Deutsche Telekom.

The consumer goods market is more evenly spread throughout the region than financial services. The UK is the biggest market, followed by France, Germany, Italy and Belgium.

Although a smaller market, Switzerland is particularly important in life sciences and financial services. Italy is described by Eduardo Antunovic of Heidrick & Struggles as a fragmented and price-sensitive market. However, medium-sized Italian companies are becoming bigger users of search and the Italian luxury goods and fashion companies that are integrating with other firms in Europe provide interesting opportunities for search firms.

According to Spencer Stuart's Manuel Marquez, one major difference between northern and southern Europe is that:

> Recruitment of independent directors is not growing as quickly
> in Spain or the rest of southern Europe as it is in the UK or
> Germany, where corporate governance reforms are pushing
> harder and the use of outside professional advice for non-
> executive director recruitment is almost a must.

Central and eastern Europe

After the destruction of the Iron Curtain between the communist-controlled economies of eastern Europe and free-market western Europe the search business got under way in eastern Europe. Throughout the 1990s, global firms poured into the region to gain a foothold and grow as demand for their services increased.

Despite the global economic downturn in the early 2000s, demand for executives in eastern Europe remained stable, reflecting the continuing investment stream from Europe and the United States into central and eastern Europe (CEE) and Russia. Since 2004, countries that have become new members of the EU such as Poland, the Czech Republic, Hungary and Slovenia have experienced an increasing demand for management talent, fuelled mainly by the need to adapt their management structures to meet the challenges of entry into the EU. Increasingly, both multinationals with operations in the region and local corporations are focusing on recruiting more local managers and relying much less on expatriates. As the quality of local managers has improved, this has become easier to do. As Sami Hamid, head of eastern Europe at Stanton Chase/Ward Howell, says:

> The new management generation in CEE is no longer second tier in terms of management education or experience. Neither is it in terms of compensation. Salary levels for local senior executives have reached expatriate compensation levels.

Countries such as Bulgaria, Croatia, Romania and Serbia are still at the beginning of a similar development. Current demand for management talent is triggered mainly by small and cautious western investments. Russia has been and still is a booming market for executive talent from both East and West. To compete internationally, Russian companies are hiring people with skills and expertise from other countries and shaping their management structures to western standards.

The increase in executive talent throughout the region has a broad base. Retail, manufacturing, financial services, IT and consumer products are the main drivers of this development. Nevertheless, a number of international executive search firms have closed their offices in CEE and Russia in efforts to reduce costs and cut headcounts. Some firms have transformed local subsidiaries into licensed representative offices in which the licensee pays a substantial proportion of running costs as well as a fee to the search firm's headquarters. However, this kind of arrangement makes it more difficult for a search firm to ensure that con-sistent standards are maintained across all of its offices. Other firms have concentrated all their CEE activities into one office in the region, such as Vienna. This has not gone unnoticed in the local business com-munity, which maintains that in order to be effective in a local market a search firm must have a local presence. As the market improves, there will be an increase in the opening of wholly owned subsidiary offices as well as licensee operations.

Latin America

Search firms first ventured into Latin America in 1965 when Robert Taylor opened an office in Mexico for Boyden, expanding into Brazil the following year. In 1970 Taylor set up his own firm TASA (Taylor Associ-ates SA), which was a leading player in the region until it was acquired by Heidrick & Struggles in the mid-1990s. Global firms such as Korn/Ferry, Egon Zehnder and Spencer Stuart entered the region later in the 1970s with offices in Mexico and Brazil. In 1985 Egon Zehnder was the first firm to enter the Argentinian market. However, search really took off only as the Latin American economies became more open during the early 1990s. Today the largest search markets in the region are Brazil and Mexico followed by Argentina.

Search in Latin America continues to struggle, primarily because of economic and political turmoil, with currency fluctuations and unstable government, especially in Argentina and Venezuela, according to Antunovic. The improving Brazilian economy is providing some search growth in the industrial, consumer and health-care sectors. The leading firms in Brazil are Amrop Hever, Spencer Stuart, Heidrick & Struggles, Egon Zehnder and Korn/Ferry.

The Mexican market is also growing, especially the industrial sector, consumer, technology and financial services. The market leader, Korn/Ferry, has long dominated the Mexican market, followed by Egon Zehnder.

Argentina is the third largest search market in the region but it has been difficult to operate in as a result of economic uncertainty and the volatility of the currency. Egon Zehnder and Spencer Stuart dominate this market. Small search markets operate in Chile, Columbia, Peru and Venezuela.

Asia and Australasia

The Asia and Australasia region may represent less than 8% of the global search market in terms of revenue, but Charles Tseng, president of Korn/Ferry Asia, forecasts that in the long term, the emerging markets of this region represent the greatest opportunity for the search profession. The regional outlook is positive, as the momentum many firms seized in 2003 and an increase in assignments have combined to provide a measure of optimism. Average growth rates of more than 30% per firm are likely to continue, particularly as the growth engines of China and India are showing no signs of slowdown. However, the continued recovery of the search market depends on many external issues, including the state of the US economy, the performance of the enlarged EU market, CEO confidence in stockmarkets and geopolitical dynamics.

The leading search firms in Asia and Australasia are Korn/Ferry, Egon Zehnder, Spencer Stuart, Russell Reynolds, Heidrick & Struggles, A.T. Kearney, Boyden and Amrop Hever, as well as Asian boutiques Bó Lè (part of Stanton Chase), Executive Access and SES. Financial specialist boutiques are numerous and include Eban, Alexander Mann, Executive Access, Whitney Group, Global Sage, Pelham Search Pacific and Robertson Smart.

Asia presents a mix of old and new markets for search. The greatest potential for search firms is to be found in the developing markets of China and India, although there are also opportunities in the more mature markets of Australia, Hong Kong and New Zealand.

The Australian and New Zealand markets experienced strong growth when many Asian markets were affected by the late 1990s economic downturn. Although Australian industry is generally more domestically focused, the export-based sectors in the mining and minerals industries recruited heavily during this period. Hong Kong and Singapore benefited from the recovery in financial services in 2004, with particular growth in investment banking, debt capital markets and private equity. After several years of decline, and in contrast to the West, the Asian technology sector also bounced back in 2004. A resurgence of recruitment needs in Singapore, which remains the hub in the ASEAN (Association of South East Asian Nations) region, was driven mainly by technology, although the asset and other financial management markets were also robust.

According to Kevin Kelly, president of Heidrick & Struggles Asia, key issues in the region include building brand recognition and helping clients to understand that executive search is a retained, fee business in which the client engages the headhunter to complete the assignment in a long-term relationship, in contrast to contingency search, where a fee is paid only if a successful candidate is found. Another issue is the mismatch of client expectations. Multinational clients expect candidates of the same standard as those they see at senior levels in Europe and the United States. Candidates in these regions generally have higher professional qualifications than local candidates, especially in China. This makes "returnees" – Asian-born but western-educated or western-experienced candidates who are generally more cross-culturally sensitive and have multinational experience – particularly attractive, and demand is greater than supply.

China Executive search has grown in response to the opening up of the Chinese economy and the country's market reforms. Tseng explains that as Chinese companies go global, they need to recruit individuals who can help them to adjust to a market economy. Although traditionally Hong Kong has been the centre for executive search, the growth of mainland Chinese industries has resulted in the growth and development of executive sourcing needs in Shanghai as well as Beijing. Many multinationals and headhunters, such as Korn/Ferry, are shifting their Asian headquarters to Shanghai, which will become the hub for commercial activities in the region over the next 5–10 years. The Hong Kong executive search industry is now very much involved in finding executives for mainland Chinese businesses.

India This is one of the fastest-growing markets in Asia, with Mumbai and New Delhi being important centres for executive search. According to Preety Kumar, head of Amrop Hever India, "Even in the global downturn between 2001 and 2003, the Indian search market grew 5–6%." Technology is a strong growth sector as India becomes a software development centre and outsourcing base. The most buoyant sectors in the Indian economy are business process outsourcing and other outsourcing, engineering and manufacturing, IT, pharmaceuticals and health care.

Middle East This is one of the least developed search markets, but according to Haider Shaif, head of the Middle East region at Egon Zehnder, there are good opportunities, especially in Saudi Arabia, Kuwait and the United Arab Emirates (notably Dubai but also Abu Dhabi), and in Qatar, Bahrain and Doha. In the longer term there are opportunities elsewhere too, but retained search in the Middle East is fraught with difficulties. For example, in Lebanon there are restrictions on bringing in foreign expatriates, and in Egypt clients are reluctant to pay retainers as they are used to contingency arrangements.

Egon Zehnder has the most established presence in the Middle East, with offices in Dubai, Jeddah and Tel Aviv, although up until 1990 the region was covered by its Istanbul office. Experience in the Middle East has taught staff at Egon Zehnder that they need to encourage clients to be real partners, and to play an active role during the entire search process. Typical problems encountered include a change in the client contact person, which disrupts the process, or the client not reading the brief. In the Middle East it is crucial that an individual consultant, rather than the firm, establishes a good personal relationship with the client – if a client likes, respects and trusts you, he will treat you as a member of his family; if he doesn't, you will probably get nowhere.

2 Using headhunters: advice for organisations

When should a company engage a headhunter?

Only engage a recruiter if you really like him or her, if the person is an expert on your market and can show evidence of a quick, accurate and effective delivery. They must be able to tell you something you didn't already know.

Simon Hearn, Russell Reynolds

Companies typically engage a headhunter when they have just lost a key employee and need to find a replacement. Sometimes a headhunter is called in after a company has approached obvious candidates but failed to recruit any of them. Headhunters believe they know the market and are in the best position to approach attractive candidates directly. However, they admit that their greatest value is in providing insight into which candidates would be most open to an offer. They can probe more deeply to find out whether a candidate really is interested in moving. Andrew Lowenthal, a partner and head of the financial services practice at Egon Zehnder, explains:

> The art of the good executive search firm is not only to know
> all the potential candidates but, more importantly, to know
> their motivations, what sort of position might attract them,
> and to be able to assess if the fit is right.

Headhunters generally know a broad range of people, and if a search is being conducted discreetly (for example, when a client does not want its own staff to know about it), a third party such as a headhunter is essential. The more senior the position, the more inclined companies are to engage a headhunter. Many companies advertise their middle-management posts and in some cases have created their own in-house recruitment teams to find less senior staff.

Companies are also more likely to engage a headhunter when they do not have the knowledge a search firm has of, say, a niche or highly specialised market. As Steve Smith of Odessa International explains:

> Good talent in the market will make itself known to the global,

most respected search firms, and speciality practice groups are a good idea. The consultants develop a network of outstanding individuals in a particular sector or industry ... We actually hired three candidates even though we were only looking for one – the calibre of talent was outstanding.

SOONER RATHER THAN LATER

Speaking on behalf of many headhunters, Tim Cook, a partner at Egon Zehnder (London), recommends that you should engage a headhunter sooner rather than later. However, the nature of the assignment may dictate exactly how and when you can start work:

I have one at the moment where we agreed with the client that we should interview those who report directly to the position we were going to search for. This achieved two objectives: it gave us a good idea of which key areas to focus on for the incoming candidate (in terms of work priorities and relationships); and it helped achieve some buy-in for the search from the managers. I have another client who has just merged two factories in different parts of the country, which has resulted in lay-offs and the launch of a post-merger integration project. He himself wants to leave but can't tell the workforce in case the post-merger project fails. He has employed us very early on so that we can start desk research, but we can't visit the operation or talk to anyone until he has made his own position clear.

Best practice is to have a good, long-term relationship with a search firm (and for large organisations, two or three firms). The ideal relationship between a company and a search firm is one in which they openly discuss the firm's succession planning, such that the search firm is aware in advance of potential hiring needs and, as well as undertaking specific assignments, can undertake "anticipatory search". Peter Wright of Estée Lauder cannot understand how a headhunter can represent its clients if it is not invited to their internal succession-planning meetings. Only by being totally involved can a headhunter think strategically and be able to consider which key employees might be vulnerable, and who might be on the firm's wish list of candidates.

In choosing a headhunter there are several important criteria to bear in mind. Does it make a difference if the headhunting firm is publicly or privately owned? Are bigger firms better? How many firms should you employ? Should you select according to individual consultants or the firm in general? What is the price of this service? Is there any scope for negotiation?

WHEN DO HEADHUNTERS GET IT RIGHT?

A headhunter can prise the key candidate out of Tesco to join you at WH Smith. He can be your guerrilla mercenary.

Virginia Bottomley, Odgers Ray & Berndtson

Here is a selection of headhunters' views on what they need to do to get it right:

- The individual doing the search should be the one who has the closest relationship with the client. Searches sold by one person and done by another rarely get done properly.
- Headhunters get it right when there is empathy between them and the client, so that they really want to work for the client through thick and thin. No one likes criticism and most headhunters have a strong sense of when a particular search is beginning to go sour.
- Headhunters should not have too many assignments on the go at once. If they do have other searches pending, these should be at different stages of the search life cycle, which is typically:
  - define the universe of qualified candidates and meet the client to discuss (2–3 weeks);
  - approach and meet the candidates (2–3 weeks);
  - present candidates to client (1–2 months).
- Headhunters get it right when they have a thorough knowledge of the client, are well briefed, know the marketplace and the candidate pool, and have the time to be thorough and systematic.
- Headhunters get it right when they take the time to find valuable references – not the former colleague or personal friend suggested by the candidate, but industry experts known to the search firm. For example, when one headhunter was undertaking a search for the head of tax for a bank, his first calls were to several senior tax lawyers who were able to rank the candidates effectively.
- The headhunter and the client should establish a rigorous time frame and stick to it.

◪ Headhunters should visit the location of the post to be filled and get a feel of the culture so that they are able to describe the working environment to the candidate (and therefore help to sell it). This will also help them decide whether a candidate is right for the environment.

How to select a headhunter

When choosing an executive search firm, focus on the quality of delivery: the economics of search have more to do with getting value than the cost of the service itself. The right placement will provide huge added value, whereas a mistake can result in serious losses for a company.

Manuel Marquez, Spencer Stuart

Choosing a search consultant is the most important part of the process and yet potential clients frequently make basic errors, according to Stephen Bampfylde of Amrop Hever, London. There are two mistakes that he witnesses time and again:

> Firstly, how often does a client visit a search firm's offices to meet the staff and "feel" the atmosphere? Instead they tend to sit in their own space and invite smooth-talking salesmen to convince them of their own worth. How much better, for example, to meet some genuine research staff (not every search firm actually has any of their own). Secondly, never ask a search professional where they are going to look or what ideas for people they have before giving them a full briefing. And certainly mistrust any that give you a quick answer. Would you believe a doctor who gave you the prescription before doing the diagnosis?

The most important criteria

The following list of criteria to consider when selecting a headhunter was drawn from discussions with HR directors at major organisations and headhunters:

◪ **Expertise.** Does the headhunter understand your business, the job, the culture, the organisation, the market?
◪ **Ambassadorial ability.** Does the headhunter represent your company well in the marketplace? Does the consultant tell the

story in such a compelling way that the candidate cannot help but want to join your company? The headhunter must be a good ambassador for your company.

■ **Reputation.** Does the headhunter have a reputation for high-quality work?

■ **Speed.** How sure can you be that the headhunter will act with the desired speed, bearing in mind what you can realistically expect if the job is to be done well? For example, for a senior appointment, will the headhunter provide a shortlist in one month and complete the search in 3–5 months?

■ **Communication.** Will the headhunter report every week and keep you informed about progress?

How do you evaluate the headhunter on these criteria? Talk to those who have used the headhunter and to other headhunters about a consultant's knowledge and track record in the marketplace – that is, the number of successful placements he or she has made. One way to assess market knowledge is to ask for a preliminary proposal letter in which the target firms are outlined. This proposal will help assess how creatively the consultant thinks in terms of where to look and whether he has understood what type of individual is needed for a successful fit.

Make sure that the consultant you choose is the person who will do the search. In large firms, assignments may be passed on to a junior associate. You can make sure that the search consultant you select actually does the assignment by making this a requirement in the proposal letter from the search firm.

Public or private firms

Some HR directors think that the ownership of the firm is irrelevant to the process of executive search and the results it achieves. Others worry – and some believe – that stockmarket pressure makes publicly listed firms focus more on the short than the longer term. One HR director commented:

> Public versus private is not important, however, public firms must demonstrate that they keep reinvesting in the business. I have not been disappointed so far but this is a concern.

Russell King, executive vice-president, group HR and business development, at Anglo American, believes it is more than a concern:

> *The partnership ethos has disappeared from some of the big*
> *public firms and intellectual capital is deserting them. Some of*
> *the private firms have more continuity and are trying harder to*
> *develop their long-term client–management relationships.*

Global or boutique firms

There is a belief among many HR directors that niche firms, or specialised boutiques, are more on the ball, have better market knowledge and show more dedication to the client. Smith complained:

> *The global firms have lost contact with the market. They are*
> *trying to do too much, thus losing added value, and they do not*
> *approach every assignment with the same energy and*
> *enthusiasm.*

However, if an assignment requires a multicountry search, there is agreement that large firms with an international reach will be more effective, as they have consultants based around the world and teams of industry specialists that can efficiently carry out a search in many countries at the same time. Others feel it is a matter of horses for courses and depends upon the assignment. Carol Scambler, head of human resources at State Street Bank & Trust in Edinburgh, explains her firm's approach:

> *We have global, European and local assignments. For an*
> *Edinburgh assignment, we would use a small UK firm with*
> *local contacts and the ability to perform market*
> *benchmarking. There is room for both: the global firms with*
> *their geographic reach; and the specialised boutiques which*
> *have depth and are often innovative and actively engaged with*
> *the client.*

Clearly, who you use should depend on the nature of the search and the culture of the company.

How many firms to use

In good times, investment banks have retained as few as two and as many as 50 headhunters with little centralisation. However, things have changed and most companies retain fewer firms than in the past. One reason is that they have become more cost conscious. Another is that one firm is thought by many HR directors to be enough for top-level assignments when you are "fishing in a limited pool". However, some global companies still feel the need to have a choice of headhunters, saying the ideal number is two or three. King admitted:

> *Although we may appear quite indiscriminate – we retain*
> *three global firms as well as three or four small boutiques –*
> *each firm is targeted with a specific niche.*

BG (formerly British Gas), an energy company based in the UK, uses a group of search firms – consisting of three global firms, two boutiques and one mid-market firm – that are retained on a continuous basis. The group, which is known as The Resource Alliance, meets regularly with BG and the headhunting firms are expected to work together.

The UK Civil Service uses about 20 search firms. As John Barker, director of Talent in the UK Cabinet Office, says, it likes "to give people a rest – they can get too close". For example, if it has recruited three lawyers through one search firm, it will generally switch to another firm for the next batch of recruits in order to see new people. "There is a tendency for firms to keep sending you the same candidates within their database."

Individual consultant or firm

What is more important: the individual consultant you work with or the firm? The consultant is, of course, of crucial importance. According to Mark Linaugh, chief talent officer at Ogilvy & Mather International/WPP:

> *One can tell the difference between good and great – a good*
> *consultant fills the spec and gets the job done, but a great*
> *consultant really cares personally that the candidate succeeds*
> *in the role and their follow-up is dedicated to making sure that*
> *this happens and not who else can they place in the firm.*

However, you should not lose sight of the firm and its reputation because it can be a powerful recruiting tool. This is why most global search firms are trying to strengthen their brands as they build their organisations internationally. It is also why wholly owned integrated firms have a powerful advantage in the marketplace compared with loosely structured networks that use different names on a local basis. So although the consultant comes first, the global reach of an organisation is also crucial, as are its research and support capabilities. Of course, star consultants have powerful persuasive powers to lure senior executives out of their firms. Also, in terms of attracting the best, most qualified candidates, a small boutique can have just as powerful a brand name as a global firm in its sector. However, this is likely to be only in respect of a particular country or region, as such firms rarely have a global reach.

Price
Fees are calculated on a percentage basis or a fixed fee based on the complexity of the assignment. Percentage-based fees may be capped with a maximum amount payable set in advance. Fees can also be fully retained: typically one-third payable at the onset of the search, one-third payable after 30 days and the final third payable after 60 days. Or they can be part on retainer, part on shortlist and part upon completion. There is plenty of room for negotiation.

Similarly, expenses can be calculated in three ways:

- a flat charge that differs according to each assignment;
- a percentage of the retainer (5–15%);
- a percentage of the total fee.

The global firms charge itemised expenses such as travel, entertainment and couriers on top of the flat charge whereas smaller firms are more likely to include travel within expenses.

Price should never be the most important factor in a decision to engage a headhunter. "Both client and search firm must be fair and flexible," says Smith. There is also a degree of comfort in "paying a small premium and getting a superior service", as King confirmed:

> *Price is the last thing we get to. Flexibility is key in the way the search is conducted. In one instance, we only paid the search firm to go to the long-list stage and not to approach candidates. This worked well for us.*

However, the majority of companies have become more cost conscious in dealing with search firms as they have with other service providers. There is constant pressure on fees and search firms are increasingly asked to be flexible on how they structure the deal. As Linaugh says:

It is hard to justify paying a significant premium if other global competitors are more flexible. Search firms need to be less wedded to custom and more in tune with the competitive pricing in the market. However, we first select a firm on capability; price is second.

How to maximise the relationship with your headhunter

Search firms must transform themselves from transaction-based vendors to trusted advisers, and develop close personal relationships with their clients. This is the key to maximising the relationships.

Bob Damon, Korn/Ferry

For a successful outcome, both the headhunter and the client must work hard at ensuring the relationship runs smoothly. You should give the headhunter as much information as possible about your company and the post. Explain why the role may be difficult to fill. Be clear and provide explicit milestones and benchmarking criteria to evaluate performance. Identify success criteria and treat the headhunter as part of your own team. As Nicholas Maupin, HR director at Cap Gemini, says:

Develop an ongoing close relationship. The headhunter should never disappear for one month and come back with a shortlist. This is a recipe for disaster.

Because so many searches commence after a key employee has departed, speed is often seen as crucial. This leads to a search for candidates who are available and are what is known as "front of mind". However, it is far better to conduct a systematic analysis of the market, including alternative or "out of the box" ideas, which can lead to a better solution. Provided the consultant really knows the market, a thorough review of a long list of candidates usually leads to a better shortlist and appointment.

Headhunters know only too well when an assignment fails because their client has not been sufficiently committed to the process. If a client is to ensure a successful relationship with a headhunter it is using, the advice that those in the search industry would give is as follows:

- Be focused with a clear idea of what you want to achieve and a precise, consistent picture of the ideal candidate. Mixed messages are unproductive.

- Be decisive about the relevant candidates. These are usually presented in two stages:
  - long list, a mapping of who's who in the sector;
  - shortlist, 6–10 ideal candidates (who are qualified, fit the brief and are potentially interested).
- Do not treat the headhunter as a supplier of bodies. There should be a real partnership based on openness and trust.
- Make sure that there is good communication between those who will decide who to hire, the human resources department and the headhunter. The executives who will ultimately make the hiring decision must be clear about the qualities, skills and personality they are looking for; the HR director's role is to ease the process; and the headhunter needs to manage the relationship between the company and the candidate. This will vary depending on the seniority of the post being filled: with junior executives, the company is buying and the candidate is selling; with senior executives, the company is selling and buying and the candidate is buying as well as selling. The headhunter, the company and the candidate should operate as a smooth-working and effective triumvirate.
- Show sincere interest in the search and do not simply outsource it to the headhunter. If confidential reports are provided, read them. Make sufficient time available for interviews and think through what questions you want to ask. Communicate to the relevant people within your firm that the search is a top priority.
- Give the headhunter plenty of access to your management team and the company workplace so that the consultant can fully appreciate the culture, the people, the challenge of the job and what skills and personality traits the jobholder will need. The more access the consultant has, the better able he or she will be to propose suitable candidates.
- Be clear about who has responsibility for the project in your company so that all communication is focused and efficiently managed.
- Give prompt and thorough feedback on the candidate. If the headhunter has got the profile wrong, provide feedback to allow changes to be made promptly. It is also unprofessional not to provide candidates with feedback or to make them wait too long for it.
- Use one search firm for an assignment. Employing two (or more) will lead to confusion in the marketplace and will send mixed

signals if candidates are approached by two firms for the same job.

- ◪ Reach hiring decisions quickly. Do not get bogged down in discussions about terms and conditions. Agree the terms swiftly and then follow up in writing. The candidate will not be impressed with your company if this part of the process drags on, and you may even lose him or her.
- ◪ Keep on top of the headhunter, but do not be overbearing. Ask for updates and say clearly when you want progress reports. Make sure you have regular meetings and make your headhunter feel part of the team.

HR directors who believe in establishing a long-term relationship with a search firm suggest that the senior partner of the search firm should be treated as one of the internal team. Search consultants believe that the relationship should go beyond a transactional approach to one of trusted adviser. According to Peter Wright of Estée Lauder:

> Good headhunters who are deeply steeped in their markets on a global level can add real business benefit beyond search. They can give you a people-based competitive view of the market. They can provide valuable insight into new business areas, particularly the way organisations structure their overall approach and, of course, compensation trends. Good headhunters should be keen to build long-term relationships. They should also be able to provide helpful insight and feedback even on your own organisation. If this advisory service can be provided combined with consistent delivery on quality searches, then surely this must be worth nurturing.

Russell King takes a similar view, describing the best relationship as:

> [When] the headhunter knows the client really well, and acts as a strategic resource, for example, how to set up a business in India or how to deal with diversity requirements in the US. Also the search firm takes the time to talk to you about the ongoing search on a weekly basis and you don't feel you are paying every time you call – as you do with a lawyer!

WHEN DO HEADHUNTERS GET IT WRONG?

Failure is lack of communication, the process not managed well, the HR director or team has to chase the headhunter. Success is an outstanding consultant who quickly understands the business environment and culture, is well known and respected in the market and his calls are always taken, he reports back quickly, and there is no problem with fees.

Mark Linaugh, Ogilvy & Mather International/WPP

Executive search can go wrong for all sorts of reasons. Eric Salmon's Anthony Harling provides examples of when headhunters get it horribly wrong and describes some of the warning signs:

- The headhunter does not understand the brief and cannot sell the story to the candidates. The search consultant must thoroughly understand the client's business.
- Communication is lacking and the client does not know what is going on during the assignment. The consultant disappears and comes back 60 days later with a totally inappropriate set of candidates.
- The headhunter does not listen properly to the client's needs. He or she focuses on certain aspects, ignoring others that are more important.
- The headhunter has insufficient sector or industry knowledge. His initial research is superficial and he relies exclusively on his existing database instead of actively researching 50–100 candidates.
- The headhunter is already overburdened with other assignments and cannot devote sufficient time to the search. A consultant should have no more than five or six active searches going on at the same time. Ask your consultant how many active searches he is working on.
- The headhunter should not have accepted the assignment in the first place. For example, the consultant knows little about the industry sector but desperately wants to work for the client.
- The client puts pressure on the headhunter to complete the task quickly. Realistically, a search for a senior executive will take a minimum of 3–6 months.
- The headhunter is not open about problems that will occur during the search. For example, if the client has a poor reputation in the market, it will be difficult to attract top candidates. Or the client may be unwilling to pay a realistic level of compensation for the type of candidate being sought.
- The headhunter takes on a job in one country but the search is to be conducted by its office in another country whose share of the fee is not enough to motivate it to work hard on the search.

☑ The headhunter is overconfident or overly optimistic. Be wary if the headhunter does not anticipate any problems.

Other services offered by headhunters

If you are about to search for a senior executive, headhunters may advise that you should conduct a management audit in advance of the assignment. They may recommend all sorts of other services too, such as coaching, training and benchmarking of staff (see below). But are they the best positioned firms to provide such services?

Some companies use headhunting firms only for search because they think they are not qualified to perform other services. For example, Carol Scambler says:

> *What do they know about coaching or assessment? We go to the experts for management assessment or coaching. Search consultants are trained to be good headhunters, to know the markets and organisational cultures well. Other services can become a distraction for the search firm.*

Such companies go to specialists for other services, perhaps Hay Group for management assessment or Penna for coaching.

However, research conducted by both Korn/Ferry and Heidrick & Struggles indicates that their clients do want them to perform other services in the field of human resources. And some HR directors will use headhunters for jobs other than search. For example, Whitehead Mann's The Change Partnership has been praised by HR directors for its executive coaching work. But, as several HR directors noted, it is marketed as a separate group and "we don't really associate it with Whitehead Mann's search division".

The problem is that many search firms have not yet convinced their clients that their related services are of the same standard as their search activities. As Mark Linaugh confirmed:

> *I am sceptical. I would prefer to go to a specialist in the field. Hanging out a shingle is not enough.*

Sometimes a search firm will introduce a new service such as assessment, and then change its mind and suspend the operation. Search firms can be entrepreneurial and faddish, and they may not really commit to building the new service if it is not core to their practice. In contrast, some search firms are deeply committed to their related services. Egon Zehnder has made a commitment to its management appraisal business and every consultant in the firm is trained to conduct appraisal in a consistent style.

A further concern is that the new services may represent a conflict of interest. If a consultant gets too involved with a client, he may lose his independence. There are various examples of what might constitute a conflict of interest and David Lord provides this one, from the candidate's perspective. A lawsuit was filed against one major firm by an unsuccessful candidate who said the firm conducted an assessment of him, found him lacking, then won the search assignment to replace him. It therefore had an interest in finding him unqualified to be promoted.

Management assessment

According to Gerry Roche of Heidrick & Struggles, all things being equal, the best candidate is always an internal candidate. This is good advice, but many firms want an independent opinion on how their internal team compares with others in the market. This is where management assessment, in which individuals and teams (including boards) are assessed for specific roles, can be used. Some search firms rely heavily on their databases to do this; others use a combination of databases, reference checking, psychometric tests, 360-degree feedback, market information and judgment.

The European market pioneered the development of management assessment, with Egon Zehnder arguably leading the way. This was partly because in Europe psychometric testing has been used in selection since the 1920s, but in the United States it did not become common until more recently. Assessment is now being offered by many search firms around the world.

Triggers or catalysts for management assessment include the following:

- acquisition and the need for an assessment of a new team;
- divestiture and the need for a review of the management team;
- succession planning talent review to assess senior managers and benchmark against the external market;
- new CEO requiring an assessment of his management team.

According to Ben Cannon, partner in leadership services at Heidrick & Struggles in the UK, some organisations have remarkably little information about their senior people and their suitability for more senior roles. This means that some talented people may not be considered for jobs that they would be good at and which are given to less well-suited people. While companies want to know whether they have the best possible leadership team, their boards are also demanding greater rigour and transparency in succession. But, Cannon warns, assessment is not an end, it is a means by which to guide decisions. Imagine going to a dentist with toothache, having an x-ray, being told "yes, you have a cavity" and then being handed an invoice. Assessment is like an extensive x-ray. The information gained should be used not only to help in selection choices (as in a merger or acquisition), but also to provide input to succession plans, leadership development and even organisational change.

Many global search firms conduct management audits including Heidrick & Struggles, Egon Zehnder, Korn/Ferry and Russell Reynolds. At Egon Zehnder, the appraisal service is well established with all search consultants in the firm trained in the assessment model. Assessment accounts for almost 20% of the firm's revenue and is a growing service. Russell Reynolds started its assessment service in 2003 with a model that includes psychometric testing. There is a small core team of dedicated assessment consultants who work alongside a regular search consultant. The process involves competency-based behavioural interviews and Russell Reynolds hopes the service will grow to 10-15% of total revenue. Spencer Stuart conducts what it calls "talent management", which includes assessment for succession planning. It is HR led and typically involves assessment of the top 100 managers, helping the HR department to identify high-potential players and to manage their careers.

Board review

This is an interactive process in which every board member is interviewed. The aim is to find out what is really happening in terms of the group dynamics of the board and determine how to make it work more effectively. Spencer Stuart led the way into this area. In the UK, other well-known firms conducting board reviews include Egon Zehnder, Heidrick & Struggles, Korn/Ferry, Whitehead Mann and a number of boutiques such as Zygos Partners, Garner International and 33 St James's.

Since the corporate scandals of the early 2000s there has been increasing pressure on boards to improve their performance. Board review has become big business in the United States and the UK, but until 2002 it was not practised in the rest of Europe, where boards were still selected through "old boy" networks. Now the board review process is growing in Europe, particularly in Germany.

Executive coaching

According to Lore International Institute, a professional development company (which has an alliance with Heidrick & Struggles), coaching helps people learn more about themselves and change their behaviour. The firm defines a coach as someone "who helps others develop their knowledge and skills and improve their performance through individual assessment and guidance". So, in effect, it is a mix of teaching, counselling and mentoring.

Coaching is commonly used by organisations at times of fundamental strategy change, when new teams are created, or to accelerate strategic imperatives. Examples of events that might result in the use of coaching are mergers and acquisitions, restructuring, privatisation or succession planning. Coaching can be for individuals or groups. It is used for individuals particularly when they have been promoted or are entering a new firm or division, or after a merger. Coaching teams are divided into "white coats" (psychologists and psychotherapists) and "suits" (consultants with diversified business experience including HR and line management).

Coaching falls broadly into four categories:

- Performance coaching is designed to enhance the success of individuals. It can include assimilation of new or transferred executives, aligning personal images to external presence and role requirements.
- Competency coaching is used to adapt and augment skills for changing requirements and to help individuals achieve their highest potential.
- Team coaching involves working with senior leadership and boards to maximise performance, redefine work roles and ensure cohesion and consistency.
- Career and life balance coaching – the fastest-growing coaching discipline – is designed to assist executives to balance the demands of work and personal lives, evaluate growth opportunities and determine career paths.

Executive coaching began in the 1980s in the United States, where the market was and still is mainly composed of lone practitioners. More recently there has been an upsurge in demand for coaching, partly because it is a natural adjunct to assessment and partly because of the need to assimilate new placements in their first 100 days, and search firms have been experimenting with different ways to include this activity in their portfolios.

Coaching is offered by a number of global firms either through a wholly owned subsidiary, such as Whitehead Mann's The Change Partnership, or through an arms-length alliance, such as Korn/Ferry's association with Marti Smye. The Change Partnership was established in 1993 in London and is recognised as a leader in the coaching business. It has 106 coaches, the majority of whom are based in the UK and the United States. Bird & Co, a boutique firm specialising in media and entertainment, also has a separate coaching service called The Coaching House. It conducts both individual and team or board coaching primarily for advertising, media, entertainment and more recently retail and technology executives.

The three publicly owned firms offer coaching (Whitehead Mann, Heidrick & Struggles, Korn/Ferry) and the three privately owned ones do not (Egon Zehnder, Russell Reynolds, Spencer Stuart). Russell Reynolds believes that coaching constitutes a conflict of interest and that assessment, rather than coaching, fits better in the firm's business model.

Interim management

This is the fastest-growing sector of recruitment, according to Tim Hammett of Heidrick & Struggles who explains:

> As permanent roles become shorter in tenure, candidates
> continue to seek more challenges and so interim becomes
> popular. It offers the ultimate flexibility: no courtship, no vows,
> no high divorce costs – just a relationship as long as it is
> needed.

Heidrick & Struggles and Boyden offer interim management services as do many large temporary-employment firms such as Manpower.

Middle-management recruitment, project recruitment and managed services

Among the global firms, Korn/Ferry has been the boldest in its diversification efforts. It now offers middle-management recruitment, project recruitment and managed services through its Futurestep venture. Middle-management recruitment is done using a combination of search, database tools and advertised selection. Project recruitment is used when a company wants to hire a significant number of staff. For example, when Starbucks needs to hire 50 store managers, Korn/Ferry may assist with a process whereby all store managers are hired according to consistent criteria. This can be more cost efficient for the client. Managed services, also known as outsourcing, is becoming increasingly common as companies seek to outsource some or all of their HR requirements including, but not limited to, recruitment. The consulting company will manage the HR requirement either onsite or offsite.

3 Using headhunters: advice to candidates

How to choose a headhunter

When selecting a headhunting firm, it is important to look for one which best suits your career needs. This chapter provides advice on how to attract attention through your CV and stand out from the crowd, and how to get that important first meeting with a headhunter. You should then review Chapter 4, which provides information on the overall ranking and geographic presence of the leading firms and an assessment of their strengths and weaknesses. Lastly, you can turn to Chapter 5 for a guide to some of the respected individual search consultants by sector or function and by geographic market.

There are also specialist research publications that rank executive search firms. Kennedy Information and Hunt-Scanlon in the US, and Executive Grapevine in the UK publish annual directories and rankings of the major players in the industry (see Appendix 3). Virtually all the executive search firms have websites, which provide information about services offered, short biographies of consultants by local office and by practice group, and summaries of research done by the firm. Website addresses are provided in the leading firms' profiles in Chapters 4 and 5.

The stage you have reached in your career will also have an influence on the type of firm you choose to approach. If you are a senior executive or have at least ten years' professional experience, you should target the global search firms and senior boutiques because they focus on senior-level appointments. Within these firms, you should approach the head of the sector or industry practice group that is of interest to you. Of course, if you have a personal introduction or referral from someone of interest to the search firm, such as a client or a well-respected individual, so much the better.

Candidates with five years' experience but with an unusual or outstanding CV may also be of interest to these global firms. Examples are candidates who speak fluent Mandarin or Arabic or Russian and have worked for leading multinational firms in the West, or those with turnaround experience in emerging markets.

If you are a recent MBA graduate with five or fewer years' work experience, it is better to target small niche firms that focus more on junior management. They will have different clients and different possibilities. It is also worth noting that a predominantly European firm such as Egon Zehnder may have more European clients than an American multinational such as Korn/Ferry or Heidrick & Struggles. Consider using your "new boy" network (see below). There may be a search consultant focusing on your industry who is an alumnus of your university or business school, or who worked for the same company as you. This person is more likely to respect your educational and career choices to date.

How to attract attention in your cover letter and CV

Egon Zehnder receives 250 unsolicited CVs each week. Other search firms receive just as many or more. Egon Zehnder staff claim to read all the CVs and then decide if they want to see people or not. This section contains advice from headhunters on how you can make sure that you get their attention. However, remember that a headhunting firm's reason for seeing a candidate is driven by a variety of factors. For example, the firm may have a particular search under way that seems a good fit, or the candidate may have worked at an organisation that the headhunter would like to know more about, or there may be something about the candidate that is particularly interesting. Egon Zehnder's Tim Cook adds another reason:

> We are always on the lookout for up-and-coming talent, and, horror of horrors, we may even approach people to work for us as a consultant.

Keep the cover letter short and straightforward

Headhunters generally read the CV first and then – if they are interested – the cover letter. It is helpful if the cover letter provides a one-paragraph summary of why you are sending in a CV. Check that you know who you are sending it to, rather than adopting the vague approach of "Dear recruiter". The cover letter should be brief – never more than one page – and:

- ◪ introduce you to the recruiter and make it clear why you are writing;
- ◪ let the recruiter know what you have to offer, such as past achievements or related skills;
- ◪ contain details of your compensation package (but only if this is asked for);
- ◪ have a strong and positive finish;

◪ convey the right impression.

Attract attention in your CV but keep it simple

Baldwin Klep of Ray & Berndtson says:

> *Create interest and speak from the heart, but don't write a self-aggrandising novel. The headhunter will probably spend no more than 30 seconds in an initial review of your CV. So the general rule should be "less is more". In other words, a succinct summary of where you have worked and what you have done is better than a 12-page autobiography. Keep it to one or two pages maximum.*

Headhunters also like to see some quantitative results included. Examples might be "grew sales by 15% and profit by 7%" or "managed a team of 300 in four locations". You are bound to be asked for figures such as these, so do not be afraid to spell out what you have achieved. If you are a consultant it is often difficult to pin down your own unique contribution to a project, so think hard about not only what projects you have been involved in but where you made a critical difference. Show mobility using evidence of your career progression and that you have made excellent choices in your career to date. Convey evidence of an ambitious candidate who is hungry for success.

TOP CV TIPS

- ◪ Keep your CV brief. Follow the classic chronological style of one or two pages citing the facts of your education and previous work experience. If you are more senior, professional experience comes first.
- ◪ Avoid wordy introductory paragraphs that tell the reader all about you. Let your experience speak for itself and understand that "time is money" for the reader.
- ◪ Do not summarise your core competencies; that is the headhunter's job.
- ◪ Quantify your achievements.
- ◪ Highlight well-known names you have been associated with, whether it is Harvard Business School, McKinsey or Goldman Sachs.
- ◪ Avoid lengthy lists of personal interests – two or three are fine.

Opinions are divided on the inclusion of photographs. Cook points out:

> Some of us love them as an aide-mémoire, others hate them.
> It's your call, but unless you are one of the tiny handful out
> there who consider themselves to be photogenic I would avoid
> them.

Do not forget to put some personal information at the end of your CV. This can bring a person to life. But whatever you do, be truthful. Cook warns:

> I met a candidate who had removed five years from his CV to
> make him appear younger. Unfortunately it just made
> everyone suspicious of him, and the client refused to see him.

Structuring a CV

There are two basic CV structures: the chronological and the skills-based.

Chronological or time-based CVs give details of each post you have held, starting with the most recent and working backwards. This is the format preferred by most employers and search consultants, and it is useful to emphasise steady career progress. It is suitable for demonstrating growth in a single profession and for anyone who has not suffered too many job changes or periods of unemployment. It may not be ideal for someone just out of school with very little work experience and/or for someone looking to change career.

The skills-based or functional CV, also known as a core-competency CV, focuses on the professional skills you have developed over the years rather than on when, where or how you acquired them. It does not emphasise dates, sometimes to the point of exclusion. Job titles and employers play a minor part in this type of format. Attention is always focused on the skill rather than the context or time. Most search consultants take a dim view of these skills-based CVs, considering that they are often a way to hide a patchy work history. However, it can be a useful format if:

- ◪ you are changing careers and want to emphasise your transferable skills;
- ◪ you are a recent MBA graduate with little work experience;

◪ you have worked for a large number of employers and wish to summarise your experience without stressing all the job-hopping;

◪ you have had a career break and are currently unemployed;

◪ you are applying for a job demanding skills that you possess but have not used in recent posts.

There are several popular "how to write a CV" books that recommend you structure your CV based upon core competencies. Core competencies cover various traits such as leadership, intelligence, charisma, strategic thinking, commercial awareness. Headhunters say you should avoid a competency-based CV. It takes too long to write and will probably not be read, and you may have to go through it all again in a competency-based interview with the headhunter (see What do headhunters look for? on page 63). "Do not list them!" warns Tim Hammett of Heidrick & Struggles. He says that the search consultant likes to determine what your core competencies are in an interview and that the required competencies will change from assignment to assignment. A charismatic, caring individual may be ideal for some posts, but not where an analytical turnaround specialist is required. The chronological CV is therefore more attractive to headhunters.

Show logical career progression and good choices in your CV

A candidate should aim to present a solid and consistent career path that shows good judgment and balance. Headhunters are often suspicious of candidates who move around and change jobs too often (every one or two years, say), in contrast to candidates who are more loyal to one organisation. However, corporate loyalty varies by industry and the economic environment. For someone working in the internet start-up sector, changing jobs every one or two years may have been the norm during the dotcom boom. Or a candidate may have followed his mentor to another firm, particularly in investment banking or advertising. If you have moved around a fair amount, you need to explain why. Virginia Bottomley of Odgers Ray & Berndtson says:

> A CV needs interpreting, a bit like Miss Marple putting the pieces together. Sometimes you need an innovator and other times a consolidator – a window breaker or a window glazier.

You may have been forced to demonstrate different leadership styles and competencies based upon the assignment. This needs to be explained.

Breadth of experience is also important. A candidate who has a good understanding of HR, marketing and finance will be of interest to a headhunter. By demonstrating wide experience and understanding, candidates increase their options dramatically.

There is a large random element in career management. Many people have been successful because they have been in the right place at the right time. However, you can make your own luck by being bold and taking opportunities that come your way. If after one or two years in a role nothing seems to be happening, push your boss for new responsibilities and experience. If these are not available, look elsewhere. As Fergus Wilson of Spencer Stuart explains, headhunters want to see well-qualified, sensible individuals who do not have unrealistic expectations but rather a mature determination to manage their career progressively.

INACCURACIES IN CVS

It goes without saying that you should make sure that the spelling, grammar and facts in your CV are correct. However, inaccuracies in CVs are common, according to a survey of human resources professionals conducted by the Society for Human Resource Management (SHRM – *Background Checks/Résumé Inaccuracies* surveys). Of 373 HR professionals surveyed, 61% say they find inaccuracies in CVs after carrying out background checks. With regard to making an offer of employment, 86% of HR professionals say that inaccuracies have a substantial influence on their decision.

A Korn/Ferry survey (*Executive Recruiter Index*, May 2004) asked headhunters to select three types of information that are most frequently fabricated or obfuscated by candidates. These are:

- reasons for leaving previous job (69%);
- results/accomplishments (68%);
- job responsibilities (45%).

Also mentioned were compensation (39%), education (24%) and dates of employment (20%). The study also looked at what kinds of due diligence clients are asking for in candidate background checks. Education verification (83%), employment verification (77%) and criminal/arrest history (35%) ranked as the top three areas.

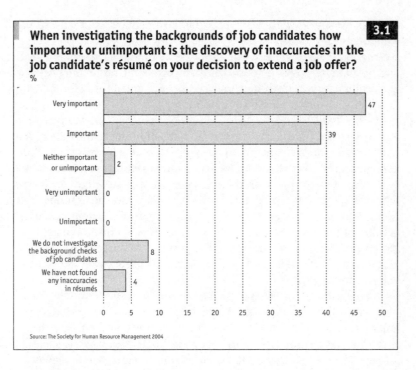

When investigating the backgrounds of job candidates how important or unimportant is the discovery of inaccuracies in the job candidate's résumé on your decision to extend a job offer? 3.1

%

Very important	47
Important	39
Neither important or unimportant	2
Very unimportant	0
Unimportant	0
We do not investigate the background checks of job candidates	8
We have not found any inaccuracies in résumés	4

Source: The Society for Human Resource Management 2004

Bob Damon of Korn/Ferry says:

Sometimes candidates are uncomfortable about having been laid off from a previous job. But rather than obfuscate or alter the reasons for leaving, it's always best to be straightforward and honest about the situation. The reality is that downsizing and restructuring have lost much of their stigma and are becoming more generally accepted by employers.

Networking tips: how to get that first meeting with the headhunter

1 Find a mentor to recommend you to the search firm

Being referred by a leading client or associate of a headhunting firm means you go straight to the top of the pile of CVs they look at. If you are American and you want to work in London, and you already know someone in the New York office, get him to refer you to his colleague in London. Peter Bassett, head of the pharmaceuticals practice at Korn/Ferry, suggests that if you work in scientific research or engineering you should give the name of your academic adviser or head of department, especially if they are well-known scientists.

2 Write to the dedicated sector practice leader

Always contact a specific person in a headhunting firm rather than the "senior partner", the "chief executive" or, even worse, the "general manager". Write to the leader in your field of interest. Russell Reynolds, for example, has more than 40 industry and functional practice groups including the following sector practice groups: consumer, financial services, health care, industrial, natural resources, technology and CEO/board services. The firm's cross-industry functional practice groups include: CFOs, legal, human resources, supply chain, marketing, chief technology officers, not-for-profit and corporate communications.

If the headhunting firm breaks the industry into subdivisions, find the right consultant within your specific field of interest. For example, you might need to write to the insurance or real estate consultant in the financial services practice; to the media or luxury/retail goods specialist in the consumer practice; or to the automotive specialist in the industrial practice group. Search consultants have had to become market intelligence experts for their clients, and the best consultant to target is the person who is an expert in your field. However, a recent MBA graduate interested in financial services might prefer to write to a junior search consultant who is in the financial services practice group and has an MBA from the same school.

3 Don't send everyone your CV

Do not write letters to several consultants at the same firm in the same local office. Make an effort to understand the organisational dynamics and structure of any search firms you approach. It is also important to understand the personal relationships among headhunters in their own organisations. If you are working with a firm that has a highly integrated sector-practice approach across markets, you should assume that the headhunter will pass on your details to appropriate colleagues. As one exasperated headhunter says, "We do talk to each other."

If you really want to talk to both the practice leader of financial services and the practice leader of technology, try one consultant first and then the other at a later date. Even better, if you have had a short meeting with one, ask for a referral to the other. But do not say a consultant told you to contact another in the same firm if this is not true, as the consultant will check.

4 Use your networking potential

Increasingly, headhunters are interested in where you studied for your MBA as well as where you have worked. Smart, much-admired universities and business schools and well-respected firms with strong cultures are in vogue, not least because of the networking potential they provide. There are also a growing number of diversity networks and women's professional networks in business, the media, the arts and journalism. Increase your visibility in these new professional networks and in your marketplace. Also get mentioned in databases, on websites and in the press by attending conferences, publishing articles and speaking at industry events, for example.

5 Be straightforward and honest

Use employment gaps, mistakes or negative events as learning experiences. Make sure that you leave no gaps on your CV and be prepared to explain what you did during this time. Headhunters know that many good people are made redundant and that many firms did not survive when the dotcom boom turned to bust. If you have lost your job, explain why. Do not lie. You will be found out – that is what researchers at headhunting firms are hired to do. You have only one reputation and only one chance with a search firm.

6 Represent yourself clearly and succinctly

An awareness of what you can and want to do demonstrates self-awareness and maturity. For example, "I've got a strong marketing background in fast-moving consumer goods (FMCG) with extensive new product development (NPD) experience. I need to move on because things aren't happening fast enough where I am. I'd now like a marketing role in telecoms or another service business where I can be involved in the development of new services. This would allow me to use my NPD experience and give me exposure to another industry sector." Always seek stretch and resist the headhunters' desire to categorise you within narrow boundaries. But be as self-aware as possible about your strengths and current weaknesses.

Edward Speed of Spencer Stuart, London, advises:

Before meeting a headhunter analyse your own strengths and weaknesses, but also ask the opinion of your friends and colleagues. Be clear about the ideal elements of your next position, including the preferred sector and even the companies you would most like to join.

And Roger Rytz of Spencer Stuart, Zurich, adds:

Search consultants thrive on information. But don't overestimate their knowledge of the companies you have worked for. Be prepared to talk about the key dimensions of the company – and your specific areas of responsibility – in terms of location, size, product range, type of customers and sales channels.

7 Sell first, buy later

Headhunters look for candidates who sell themselves well. In an interview, sell first and buy later. Hook those searching for someone before you make up your mind as to whether you want the job in prospect, advises Robin Roberts of Egon Zehnder. Many do the reverse, only to discover that it is a great opportunity and that other candidates have been shortlisted. Look and act ambitious and hungry for success. "Headhunters do not want to present low-key people, losers or defeatists to their clients," says James Martin of Egon Zehnder. But do not go overboard. Headhunters also look for team players, people who genuinely put the interests of the firm they work for ahead of their own. Younger candidates who are unrealistically ambitious or overly aggressive may not play well. "Quiet confidence works best," advises Victoria Hyndmann of Heidrick & Struggles.

8 Don't talk too much – be a good listener

According to a survey of MBA candidates conducted by Korn/Ferry in 2001, 43% of recruiters say the most common interview mistake is to talk too much. It also found that 33% of recruiters say candidates are unprepared and 24% say MBA graduates have overinflated egos. Candidates should quickly hook the consultant with a brief overview of their strengths and why they stand out, and then listen carefully to what the job really involves, the key drivers, the culture of the firm and what is important to the company.

9 Be helpful to the headhunter

If you can provide an extra set of eyes and ears in your field of expertise and help your headhunter find other candidates or clients, the headhunter is likely to want to pull out the stops in helping you. According to Hammett, you are helping each other and this will be the start of a productive and hopefully long-term relationship.

"Be helpful to headhunters. They have memories like elephants," says Gerd Wilhelm of Spencer Stuart. He confirms that if you offer helpful information on a current search, at some point, you will get in the door to see that consultant yourself. Headhunters also advise candidates to e-mail the search consultant after their meeting to summarise the key points of your discussion.

Rytz says:

> Offering to help a consultant identify the best people from your sphere of expertise and professional network is a good way to win his interest and ultimately become a candidate. Tell him what type of people you know and who you have the most easy access to and confirm that he can always call you for help.

10 Aim to build a long-term relationship

Don't be frustrated if your headhunter cannot find you the perfect job right away. Search consultants are client driven and what you want must tie in with what at least one of their clients requires. Remember also that most consultants handle only about 20 searches a year. Nonetheless, consultants can be an invaluable sounding board for career advice, market intelligence and, in the long term, they may certainly provide your dream job.

Martin Heijman of Spencer Stuart, Amsterdam, says:

> Consultants are busy and generally focused on current assignments. Building a relationship with a consultant should always involve positive contact: sharing information, asking advice, or informing the consultant when you are a candidate on another firm's assignment. Promote the value of your network and pass on information about potential searches, but be careful not to irritate the consultant with over-frequent contact.

11 Differentiate yourself

Differentiate yourself from the crowd by asking questions that demonstrate your depth of market knowledge and insight. This is the best way to stand out. Companies are generally not keen on candidates who are too different – people whose appearance or demeanour is at odds with the culture of the firm. Finding the right person for a job is a great responsibility and headhunters and their clients are generally risk-averse, even if they are prepared to be adventurous. So they will want to make choices that they feel are justifiably safe.

Speed says:

> If you are seeing a headhunter about a specific opportunity
> and you know who the client is, do your preparation so you
> can ask intelligent and informed questions – and be succinct.
> Listen, make eye contact, and be sure your points have been
> understood.

12 Don't call to ask for career advice

Headhunters match individuals to jobs. They are not career advisers. They are client driven and client focused. Candidates who say they are looking for a change of career direction "make our hearts sink", confides Andrew Lowenthal of Egon Zehnder. As stated above, companies usually use headhunters to make safe bets. If a company is hiring a new chief financial officer (CFO), it wants someone who is an experienced CFO, not an ex-banker who sees only one side of the CFO's role and thinks he could do it better than his former clients. But headhunters are imaginative enough to see what jobs you might be suited for, and in some cases your CV may be transferred to another headhunter in the firm who is working on your ideal assignment.

Heijman says:

> If you are having a general conversation with a consultant, be
> as precise as possible in describing your ideal job. Be open
> about describing your strengths and qualities and always
> support your case with examples. This will make it easier for a
> consultant to put you forward as a candidate should an
> appropriate opportunity arise.

HOW TO GET NOTICED FOR NON-EXECUTIVE DIRECTORSHIPS

Non-executive directorships can differ substantially depending on whether they are for privately held, venture capital or private-equity-backed small businesses or for major publicly quoted companies. Whichever type you are targeting, one way of becoming more visible is to have people talking about you – in other words, getting recognition from your peers and observers, says Egon Zehnder's Tim Cook. This means not only doing an outstanding job but also treating your colleagues, whether senior or subordinates, with respect. Remember that there is always a chance that people you have worked with will be asked to give a reference. The most outspoken commentators in any sector are generally investors in firms. Fiercely committed and attentive, they will take their time to form impressions and then be highly vocal. They will also seek references on you through their own networks, and these might include people you have worked with.

According to Mina Gouran of Korn/Ferry, UK, there are a number of things you should bear in mind when trying to get noticed for a non-executive directorship:

- It is always easier to be noticed when you are employed in a high-powered job.
- The more visible you are the more likely you are to be noticed.
- If you are in the private sector, it can help to show you have dedicated some time to social corporate responsibility, the arts or government think-tanks.
- It can be helpful to have board experience from not-for-profit, academia, charities or professional associations of note while still in an executive role.
- Make sure your wider strategic financial and corporate skills are known or, if you have been operating in a narrow remit, make sure you develop a wider perspective.

What do headhunters look for?

When selecting candidates for their active database, headhunters look for a good mix of past experience, skills, personal attributes and core competencies.

1 Quality of education

Do you have an MBA from a prestigious school? Highly respected universities and business schools count for a lot, especially for younger candidates in the early stages of their career. The educational experience is an important differentiating factor. If you are young and do not have a lengthy track record, can you point to any distinctive achievements, such as the best thesis of your class at university, a special award, or even an outstanding achievement in sports or the arts?

2 Quality of training and work experience

Did you spend your first five years with a blue-chip firm noted for its excellent training experience? Firms that are rated for their training skills include GE, BP, Shell, Emerson, Boeing and 3M in the industrial sector; Colgate, Proctor & Gamble, Diageo, Nestlé, Gillette and Coca-Cola in consumer goods; Citigroup, Goldman Sachs and Morgan Stanley in the financial sector; Microsoft, Apple and Sony in consumer electronics; Sanofi-Aventis, Johnson & Johnson, Merck, Novartis, Amgen, Pfizer, Eli Lilly, GlaxoSmithKline and Bristol Myers Squibb in health care; Marriott and Four Seasons in hospitality and leisure; McKinsey, Bain, Boston Consulting Group and Booz Allen Hamilton in consulting.

3 Achievement

Attractive CVs are rich with numbers; for example, "cut costs by 25%", "increased revenue by 15%", "responsible for a sales team of 500" or "increased profits by 15%". This gives the consultant a real sense of your accomplishments and the size of projects or teams that you have managed. Don't be vague on your CV. It is the first impression a headhunter gets of you and is therefore of crucial importance.

Speed says:

> When discussing your achievements or experiences you must explain their direct relevance to the position at hand. Don't merely describe what you have done as though you were acting in isolation, but describe how you did it and the impact of your actions on others.

ADVICE FOR MBA GRADUATES

If you went to one of the leading headhunters, what advice would they offer you as a recent MBA graduate? Which sectors should you consider and why? The following are responses to these questions posed in 2004 from CEOs and senior executives of leading headhunting firms.

> I wouldn't recommend a specific sector over another. But what I do

recommend is that, to make it easier to be hired, graduating MBAs ought to pick a sector of interest and obtain an intimate knowledge of it. First jobs are more important than ever. New MBAs often make the mistake of placing too high a value on product and compensation when choosing where to work. These are important factors but I would suggest that the first consideration should be picking a good company with good people. Good people can open doors. For advice and counsel, new graduates should seek to identify mentors who have credibility in the marketplace and then use this network to its fullest extent. New graduates should be ambitious, yet also realistic with their goals. And, finally, they should always make short-term decisions with a long-term view clearly in mind.

I'd almost certainly pursue a career in the services sector. Advertising, media, strategy consulting, executive recruitment, coaching and assessment and the like are industries that are undergoing massive change at present, and therefore opportunities to be part of a new and brighter future are plentiful. In addition, these services sectors provide an opportunity not just for skill development, but for networking, exposure to multiple industries and personal advancement, which many "client-side" companies struggle to deliver.

In every sector there are always great companies with excellent performance records and above-average growth levels. Individuals should enter the sector and function in which they believe they can perform above the average, reap more enjoyment and, therefore, make more of an impact. Excellent professionals succeed by identifying and cultivating their own specific areas of expertise, rather than simply being carried forward by the average growth of their industry.

The services sector, probably media or leisure, which will have the fastest growth. A recent graduate should become an entrepreneur or else plan their résumé for the long term.

I would always advise people to follow their heart and interests; success will come and is defined in many ways.

Corporate governance or professional services. Choose a firm which has a track record of retention and development, and an international outlook. If possible, choose private rather than public.

I would not suggest any specific sector as there will always be ups and downs. More importantly, new graduates should seek employment with companies that train well, are fast and flexible, those with Six Sigma [a measure of quality] values, those that provide opportunities for employees to excel.

All sectors offer opportunities. The challenge for an MBA is to recognise which opportunity their skills can best exploit.

The pharmaceuticals/health-care or financial/professional services sectors because margins are respectable and these sectors tend to be less cyclical or counter-cyclical in some instances. Manufacturing is anticipated to experience global expansion because of growing consumerism in expanding markets.

Recent graduates should be prepared to multitask and to focus on taking real responsibility for delivery within whatever organisation they join as soon as is feasible as no one can take a delivered achievement away from you. Learn to think globally, learn at least one major foreign language if not more, be open and gain exposure to other cultures, and be prepared for global mobility. Dynamic career progression is typically based on a mix of achievements, international mobility and language skills.

If a person is looking for challenging sectors (high risk with high gain) they should consider management consulting (strategy) and certain sectors of financial services. It is a very exciting and dynamic sector; it lives close to the economic climate. When it is growing it is excellent; when it is declining it is dire. For a safer bet consider consumer products and health care.

Sector does not matter. In the short term work for a well-managed company where you will learn. Seek new experience and operate with integrity.

Jobs in new industry sectors such as technology are always more interesting than those in old industries. Pick a large international firm for your first assignment rather than an officer-level position with a smaller or early-stage company. Look for an opportunity that offers wide experience rather than a chance to go overseas immediately. However, set a goal and plan to live overseas for three years before you are 40, preferably with regional or global responsibilities, rather than one-country accountability. Promote your capabilities by developing and maintaining a network. Keep your head down and focus on the challenges of the current position rather than that elusive but attractive next position.

Based on personal desire, technology, financial services and life science offer unprecedented growth potential.

I would recommend sectors such as fast-moving consumer goods (FMCG), telecommunications, manufacturing industry. I would tell a recent graduate to choose a good solid company and go international. China and India are definitely areas where experience could prove quite positive.

We would not recommend a specific sector; it will depend on your own interest and abilities. Overall, we would underline the importance of the first job for the rest of the career, and the importance of getting international exposure in your professional activities.

Follow your heart and interests. People are good at doing what they like doing. That's the best way to success.

4 Mobility and career progression

Demonstrate that you can handle increasing amounts of responsibility and that you are loyal. Working for three different banks or advertising agencies in five years is less impressive than showing progress in one organisation over a similar period. But spending many years with one organisation may cause concern that you might not be able to adapt easily to a new opportunity. Lowenthal explains that people who have spent many years with one employer get used to a single culture and do not transfer well; they have not learned how to read different corporate cultures.

Headhunters appreciate broad sector and functional expertise as well as geographic diversity. Martin gives this example: a candidate who has spent 25 years in Houston will probably not find it easy to move to New York or Atlanta and will therefore be less attractive. The greater your breadth of experience in terms of type of role, industry sector and type of firm, the more marketable you will be. There are thousands of different companies and permutations of opportunity.

Tony Vardy of Spencer Stuart says:

> A few years ago, software firms wanted candidates exclusively
> with technical software experience. Now, clients want
> candidates with broader scope with diversified sector and
> functional expertise. Thus an ideal candidate to be a senior
> executive of a software firm might come from the broadcast,
> publishing or media world. This broadening of scope started
> with the internet revolution.

5 Competency-based skills

Many clients ask headhunters to use competency-based and/or psychometric assessment to evaluate candidates. One such model looks at the
organisation and culture of a firm as well as the role and determines
which leadership traits are most important to succeed in a particular job.
Although most of the global search firms have their own models for this,
there is much similarity among them. According to Ben Cannon of Heidrick & Struggles, when the models in common use are compared, there
is some 80% overlap in the specific competencies used. Models must be
customised to fit a company's strategy, culture, structure and values. He
adds:

> No one model is significantly better than any other, although
> there is an emerging concern among practitioners that too many
> focus too much on the soft stuff (eg, style, behaviour, people,
> change, process) and too little on the hard stuff (eg, structure,
> cost management, strategy formulation). What's important is
> that the competencies assessed are right for the client and
> relevant to the job, and that the right tool is used to make an
> objective and robust assessment of a given competence.

Many search firms evaluate candidates based on selected core competencies which change with each assignment. Typically four or five of
the competencies will be essential to a search. Ideally, candidates should
be aware of how they rate on these attributes. Evaluation of competency-based skills is done through an interview that looks for evidence
of when candidates have done these things rather than what they
would do in a hypothetical situation. Firms that use this tool have a
grading system depending on the quality of the evidence provided and
the number of examples given. A good competency interview may

cover 15 or more topics and last three hours. It can be testing for both the candidate and the consultant. One model of core competencies looks like this:

1 Planning and organising: the ability to set up and monitor timescales and plans.
2 Commercial awareness: the level of understanding of costs, profits, markets and added value.
3 Problem-solving and analysis: the ability to make systematic and rational judgments based on relevant information.
4 Leadership: the ability to motivate and empower others to reach organisational goals.
5 Quality orientation: the ability to follow through to make sure that appropriate quality and productivity standards are set and met.
6 Specialist knowledge: the level of understanding of technical or professional aspects of work and keeping up-to-date with change.
7 Persuasiveness: the ability to influence or convince others in a way that results in acceptance, agreement or behavioural change.
8 Oral communication: the ability to speak clearly, fluently and in a compelling manner to both individuals and groups.
9 Written communication: the ability to write in a clear and concise manner using appropriate grammar, style and language for the reader.
10 Creativity and innovation: the ability to identify fresh approaches and show a willingness to question traditional assumptions.
11 Action orientation: the demonstration of a readiness to make decisions, take the initiative and originate action.
12 Strategic thinking: the demonstration of a broad view of issues, events and activities and the perception of their longer-term impact.
13 Interpersonal sensitivity: the ability to interact with others in a sensitive and effective way and to work well with others.
14 Flexibility: the ability to adapt to changing demands and conditions.
15 Resilience: the ability to maintain workforce effectiveness in the face of setbacks or pressure.
16 Personal motivation: an enthusiastic commitment to work hard towards organisational and personal goals.

Where the interviewer is assessing a candidate's persuasiveness and his or her ability to convince other people to accept a new idea, typical questions that might be asked include the following:

- How do you describe your style of influencing other people? Give examples. What was the specific issue?
- Were there other ways in which you influenced people, staff, employees or management? What was the outcome?
- Describe another situation where you influenced someone.

Candidates need not be nervous about this assessment process. Indeed, many use it as a way to obtain independent and rigorous feedback about their leadership skills and potential.

6 Charismatic personality

Headhunters are looking for candidates that are articulate, present well and have excellent communication skills. The most commonly heard question in the Egon Zehnder office is: "Does he or she present well?" Another behavioural trait that endears candidates to clients is their "openness to learning". According to Egon Zehnder's Joe Haim, this means a continued demonstration of improving with every job and every new task and an eagerness to embrace new ways of doing things, not a "I know how it's done – know-it-all".

7 Honesty, integrity, good values and great references

A president of a top-ten global search firm was fired for claiming that he had a combined MBA/JD degree from Harvard when he didn't. People who lie about their credentials are usually found out, and their reputation is ruined. Candidates are also evaluated on the kind of language they use in an interview. How did they treat the reception staff and secretary at the search firm? What are their views on attracting and maintaining a diverse team? Candidates need to be attuned to these increasingly important issues. "Rankism, racism, boorish language and sexism do not play well," warns Hyndmann.

Impeccable references are essential. Most headhunters will take references before introducing candidates to clients, so be prepared. Also they will not necessarily call the people you mention; headhunters are more likely to call people whose judgment they trust and who have come across you professionally.

8 Emotional intelligence

Many search firms believe that high emotional intelligence is the biggest differentiator of attractiveness in a candidate. Emotional intelligence (EI) is a measure of interpersonal skills such as how well you handle yourself and others. Along with charismatic personality, Daniel Goleman's book *Working with Emotional Intelligence* (Bloomsbury, 1996) cites the following keys to EI, many of which are found in the core competency listing in point 5 above:

- self-awareness
- managing emotions
- self-control
- empathy
- skill in handling relationships
- motivation
- influencing
- listening
- leading
- personal reflection
- fulfilment.

According to Juliana Zinger of Egon Zehnder, a candidate with a high level of EI but a moderate level of experience will frequently beat a candidate with the opposite balance of skills. EI indicates a candidate's ability to learn and drive results through others: critical skills for any successful leader. Candidates who drive results without regard for interpersonal factors often leave bodies in their wake, and can significantly damage an organisation despite what appear to be brilliant results.

9 Breadth of experience and cross-cultural sensitivity

The greater the breadth of experience you have in terms of role, industry sector, type of firm and geographic market, the more marketable you will be. Constantly try to expand your range of experience and responsibilities. The major oil companies are now just about the only employers who create renaissance men and women. For example, BP will move its brightest and most capable managers from petroleum engineering in Aberdeen to an HR job in Angola and then to a marketing job in Chicago. Assuming someone has been successful in each position, this seemingly disjointed career path will continue up through the organisation, including at some stage the all-important head-office role, which gives exposure to the most senior management. This unusual development route gives individuals increasing confidence that they can deal with whatever is thrown at them. By their mid-40s they are well-rounded, internationally minded people who can be plugged into any gap in the organisation with the confidence that they will perform. This can happen because the company is so large that it has the infrastructure to support the individual.

For executives in smaller organisations that lack the size or flexibility to accommodate such diverse career paths, however, this breadth is more difficult to obtain, and they need to be constantly assessing their career. Getting a broader range of experience may be possible only by moving companies. Unfortunately, you may come up against the conservatism of companies which will only settle for someone who has done what they want doing. Catch 22? Not necessarily, because even though the functional role may be similar the new company culture will be different. It will have different ways of assessing plans using different assumptions, corporate communication will be done differently, and the pace of the organisation will be faster or slower. This provides breadth and valuable new perspectives that enable the executive to understand what is best business practice. As Wilson explains:

> Relatively minor techniques and ways of doing things that an
> executive has taken for granted in company A may be
> regarded as revolutionary in company B.

Headhunters are interested in people with a global outlook, who are sensitive and curious towards other countries and geopolitics. Linguistic ability is also an advantage, as is evidence of having completed successful international assignments. Speed suggests:

> If you have not had the opportunity to go on an international
> assignment, then experience in different company cultures
> helps.

And Rytz says:

> A headhunter will want to gauge how multicultural you are.
> Have you worked internationally? How many languages do
> you speak? Have you been responsible for, sold to, or
> successfully negotiated with people from different cultures?

A Columbia Business School survey in the early 2000s found that cultural understanding is the most valued leadership attribute, followed closely by people skills and communication. Globalisation is obviously one reason this is a valued trait, but another may be because cultural differences in management styles remain as pervasive as ever. Another survey (*Getting the Edge in the New People Economy*, 2004) of 700 managers in seven countries around the world, conducted for SHL, a psychometric consultancy, by The Future Foundation, a London-based think-tank, showed that managers from different countries had markedly different attitudes to their staff and their company. It suggested seven different cultural profiles in business, named according to their differentiating characteristics:

- **Go-getting.** Enthusiasm and leadership are demanded from employees. Leadership is individualistic rather than consensual, and risks are taken frequently. The business environment is highly charged, energetic and meritocratic. Example: United States
- **Worker bee.** Tasks frequently overlap, with shared responsibilities; decisions are consensual and risks are avoided. Employees are motivated by a strong sense of pride and are perfectionist and efficient. Example: Hong Kong
- **Nurturing.** Employers take good care of their staff and assist poor performers. They make sure that everyone is content in their work and that they are focused on an area in which they excel. Example: Sweden
- **Easy-going.** Workers are trusted to get on with their tasks freely and autonomously, and there is a strong emphasis on "getting the job done". Strong leadership is treated sceptically. Example: Australia
- **Stalwart.** Aversion to risk-taking, a need for solid authority figures, clearly defined roles and functions, and scepticism towards change for change's sake. The emphasis is on reliability and dependability. Example: UK
- **Mechanistic.** Managers and staff work by the book and are direct and well organised. The culture is egalitarian but includes a strong sense of individual responsibility. Example: Netherlands
- **Upfront and direct.** Direct, honest and time-aware. Managers are attentive to their workers' needs but will move them on if they have difficulties in their role. Egalitarian culture. Example: Netherlands
- **Family entrepreneurs.** Work environment is organised around the principles of a family. The boss plays a patriarchal role and authority is cascaded down with leadership functions at lower

levels too. High acceptance of authority and low tolerance of failure and underperformance. Example: India

Intercultural Business Improvement (IBI) has developed a self-assessment model to determine a candidate's level of cultural understanding. The "Intercultural Readiness Check" evaluates candidates on four intercultural competencies: intercultural sensitivity, uncertainty, communications style and the ability to build commitment (see Appendix 3). IBI says the model can be used in developing individual competences, in preparing staff for international roles and in building multicultural teams.

4 Leading executive search firms

The global firms

As Table 4.1 shows, in 2004 the top ten firms accounted for revenues of $2.2 billion, which is reckoned to be about one-third of the total market. Seven of these firms had revenues of more than US$100m and, as has been the case for more than ten years, Heidrick & Struggles and Korn/Ferry led the pack. In terms of revenue per consultant, six of the top ten firms achieved over $1m: Spencer Stuart, Heidrick & Struggles, Egon Zehnder, Russell Reynolds, Globe and Korn/Ferry. High levels of revenue per consultant usually reflect a firm having a relatively high level of high-earning search assignments for senior executives.

Ups and downs

Table 4.2 shows just how much headhunters' earnings can vary from year to year. In 2000, the top five firms made $2,098.3m. Just three years later, they made $1,414.6m, a drop of more than 30%.

Number of offices worldwide

Table 4.3 shows that in 2005 Amrop Hever with 79 offices around the world has more than any other search firm, although over half of its offices are in Europe. Korn/Ferry was not far behind with 73 offices and has a good spread among the regions. Much like Amrop Hever, Boyden's 69 offices are concentrated in Europe. Egon Zehnder has 59 offices and Heidrick has 58 offices. Russell Reynolds has the smallest number of offices of the top five global firms.

In Europe Amrop Hever and Boyden have the largest number of local offices, followed by Egon Zehnder and Transearch. All have a strong European presence.

In North America Heidrick & Struggles and Korn/Ferry have long dominated search, along with Spencer Stuart. Korn/Ferry has the largest number of North American offices, followed by Spencer Stuart and then Heidrick & Struggles.

In Latin America Amrop Hever has the largest number of offices and is well respected in the region. Korn/Ferry, Spencer Stuart and Egon Zehnder also have excellent and long-standing reputations.

In Asia and Australasia in 2004 Stanton Chase was joined by Bó Lè, an Asian regional group, which gives it the largest number of offices

Table 4.1 **Leading global executive search firms by revenue, 2004**

	Revenue ($m)	% change 2003–04	Revenue per consultant ($'000)	Number of offices[a]
Korn/Ferry	402.2[b]	29.4	1,008.0	73
Heidrick & Struggles	375.4	18.1	1,264.0	58
Spencer Stuart	362.4[c]	18.2	1,289.0	49
Egon Zehnder	335.7	23.5	1,180.0	59
Russell Reynolds	268.0	33.0	1,120.0	32
Ray & Berndtson	147.4	16.8	491.3	51
Amrop Hever	135.3	20.3	512.5	79
Globe	76.0	23.0	1,100.0	17
IIC Partners	75.3	11.3	418.3	53
Transearch	70.0	39.4	345.0	53

a 2005. b Year ending October 2004. c Year ending September 2004.

Table 4.2 **Leading executive search firms: worldwide revenue, selected years ($m)**

	1994	1997	2000	2003
Heidrick & Struggles	135.0	263.3	574.2	317.9
Korn/Ferry	169.0	301.1	567.0[a]	315.1
Spencer Stuart	130.0	229.0	362.0	306.7
Egon Zehnder	122.0	181.9	290.0	271.9
Russell Reynolds	127.0	184.3	305.1	203.0
Ray & Berndtson	69.0	117.3	176.2	126.2
Amrop Hever	96.0[b]	182.0[b]	120.0	112.5
IIC Partners	24.2	44.4	60.0	67.6
Transearch	38.6	68.0	60.0	50.0
Signium	70.0[c]	104.7[c]	55.0	43.1
A.T. Kearney	28.5	53.3	75.0	39.0

Note: Data not available for all firms.
a Year ending April 30th 2001. b Figure for Amrop International; Hever figure was $53.6m for 1997; $36.4m for 1994. c Figures for Ward Howell, renamed Signium in 1998.
Sources: Economist Intelligence Unit; search firms

Table 4.3 **Leading executive search firms: number of offices by region, 2005**

	Europe	North America	South America	Asia & Australasia	Middle East & Africa	Total
Amrop Hever	44	5	12	15	3	79
Korn/Ferry	23	23	10	15	2	73
Boyden	29	14	7	18	1	69
Egon Zehnder	28	11	6	11	3	59
Heidrick & Struggles	22	17	7	11	1	58
Stanton Chase	17	12	9	18	–	56
IIC Partners	26	12	4	11	–	53
Transearch	28	9	6	8	2	53
Ray & Berndtson	28	12	4	5	2	51
Spencer Stuart	19	17	5	7	1	49
Russell Reynolds	12	12	2	6	–	32
A.T. Kearney	12	12	1	4	–	29
Signium	14	4	1	6	–	25
ITP	6	6	–	9	–	21
Penrhyn	9	3	3	3	–	18
Globe	11	5	–	1	–	17
Highland	1	12	1	3	–	17
Whitehead Mann	9	2	–	1	–	12
Christian & Timbers	1	7	–	–	–	8
Eric Salmon	4	1	–	–	–	5

Source: Search firms

in Asia for any integrated firm or network. Boyden, a long-established player in Asia, is still well represented with 16 offices. The leading global firms in Asia and Australasia by revenue are Korn/Ferry, Heidrick & Struggles, Spencer Stuart, Egon Zehnder and Russell Reynolds.

Profiles of the leading global search firms

The 20 firms profiled in this chapter have been selected because they conduct search at the highest levels (one indicator of which is high revenue per consultant), have global appeal and are of particular interest because of recent additions to their networks. They are organised in various different ways (see pages 13–14 and 16–17):

- Integrated, publicly owned: Heidrick & Struggles, Korn/Ferry, Whitehead Mann
- Integrated, privately owned: Egon Zehnder, Eric Salmon, Highland Partners, A.T. Kearney, Russell Reynolds, Spencer Stuart
- Non-integrated, close association of locally owned firms: Amrop Hever, Boyden, ITP, Signium, Transearch
- Non-integrated, association of locally owned firms: Globe Search, IIC, Penryhn
- Combination (integrated, joint-venture associations and strategic alliances): Christian & Timbers, Ray & Berndtson, Stanton Chase

Most of the leading firms say they charge fees based on a proportion (typically one-third) of first-year salary or total compensation package.

Firms are listed according to size of revenue, from biggest to smallest. Net revenue is revenue minus reimbursed expenses. Where there is a consistent e-mail address for consultants we have given it, but where it varies from firm to firm (mainly in the case of networks) we have not. Search consultants move around, but those named in this book were working for the firms indicated when it went to press. Spellings of names have been checked where possible.

Korn/Ferry International

Senior management

Chairman and CEO . . . . .Paul C. Reilly
Presidents . . . . .North America: Robert A. Damon
                                      Europe: Chris van Someren
                                      Asia Pacific: Charles Tseng
                                      Latin America: Sergio Averbach

Board of directors

Paul C. Reilly	David L. Lowe
James E. Barlett	Edward D. Miller
Frank V. Cahouet	Ihno Schneevoigt
Spencer C. Fleischer	Gerhard Schulmeyer
Sakie T. Fukushima	Ken Whipple
Patti S. Hart	

Headquarters

North America
1900 Avenue of the Stars
Suite 2600
Los Angeles, CA 90067
US
Tel: +1 310 552 1834

Europe
123 Buckingham Palace Road
London SW1W 9DZ
UK
Tel: +44 20 7312 3100

Asia & Australasia
50 Raffles Place #28-06
Singapore Land Tower
Singapore 048623
Tel: +65 6224 3111

Website
www.kornferry.com

Office locations

Europe   Amsterdam, Athens, Barcelona, Brussels, Bucharest,
                Budapest, Frankfurt/Koenigstein, Geneva,
                Gothenburg, Helsinki, Istanbul, London, Luxembourg,
                Madrid, Milan, Rome, Moscow, Oslo, Paris, Stockholm,
                Vienna, Warsaw, Zurich

Americas	Atlanta, Bogota, Boston, Buenos Aires, Calgary, Caracas, Chicago, Dallas, Denver, Houston, Irvine, Lima, Los Angeles, Mexico City, Miami, Minneapolis, Monterrey, Montreal, New York, Philadelphia, Princeton, Quito, Rio de Janeiro, San Francisco, Santiago, São Paulo, Seattle, Silicon Valley, Stamford, Toronto, Tysons Corner, Vancouver, Washington DC
Asia & Australasia	Auckland, Bangkok, Beijing, Hong Kong, Jakarta, Kuala Lumpur, Melbourne, Mumbai, New Delhi, Seoul, Shanghai, Singapore, Sydney, Tokyo, Wellington
Middle East & Africa	Dubai, Sandton

Practice groups

Industry groups

CONSUMER

Advertising and marketing services	Retail and apparel
Consumer products	Travel, hospitality, leisure
Media and entertainment	

FINANCIAL

Alternative investments	Insurance and risk management
Asset and wealth management	Operations, technology and consumer
Corporate and investment banking	

INDUSTRIAL

Aerospace and defence	Industrial products
Automotive	Industrial services
Energy	

LIFE SCIENCES

Pharmaceuticals	Life sciences contract services
Biotechnology	Health care services
Medical devices	

TECHNOLOGY

Communications and convergence	Software and emerging technologies
Professional and IT services	Systems and electronics

Functional groups

Association, not-for-profit, government	Homeland defence security
	Human resources
Diversity	Interim management
Education	Information technology officers
External affairs	Legal
Financial officers	

Services offered

Board, CEO services
Executive search
Futurestep (middle-management recruitment)
Leadership development solutions
Management assessment
Executive coaching and development

Global performance data

Figures are for financial year ending April 30th 2004

Net revenue	$402.2m[a]
Number of partners	426
Number of researchers	350
Net revenue per consultant	$1m[a]
Number of offices worldwide	73
% change in net revenue 2003/04	29.4[a]

a Year ending October 2004.

Global net revenue by industry sector (%)

Consumer	23
Education/non-profit	5
Financial services	15
General	1
Health care	5
Industrial	23
Life sciences	10
Technology	18

81

Global net revenue by function (%)

CEO and board director	8
CFO, senior executive, general management	47
Finance and control	7
Information systems	2
Human resources and administration	8
Manufacturing, engineering, research and development, technology	8
Marketing and sales	19
Other functions	1

Net revenue by geographic region (%)

Asia and Australasia	17
Europe, Africa, Middle East	33
Latin America	10
North America	40

Comments

Korn/Ferry was founded in Los Angeles in 1969 by Lester Korn and Richard Ferry, two partners from Peat, Marwick, Mitchell & Co. During their first year they opened an office in New York, and within three years they employed 42 people in six cities in the United States. The company's first overseas office was opened in Brussels in 1972 and at the same time it established a European headquarters in London. An office in Paris soon followed as did expansion into the rest of Europe.

Korn/Ferry opened an office in Tokyo in 1973, and this propelled the firm's expansion into Asia. A merger with Sydney-based Guy Pease Associates in 1979 helped to establish a presence in Australia. Similarly, a merger with Mexico-based Hazzard & Associados in 1977 paved the way for expansion into Latin America. A 1993 merger with Brussels-based Carré Orban, a European search firm, added offices in Scandinavia and Luxembourg.

In 1998, Korn/Ferry launched Futurestep, an internet-based venture aimed at the middle-management market. It began as a low-value transactional provider of candidates, but following various difficulties it has become more relationship-oriented, offering middle-management search, project recruitment, managed services and interim solutions.

In 1999, Korn/Ferry became a public company traded on the New York Stock Exchange. Acquisitions during the late 1990s and early 2000s included Hofmann Herbold (a German full-service firm), Levy Kerson (a

New York retail and fashion specialist), Helstrom Turner & Associates (a Los Angeles retail and fashion specialist), Pearson, Caldwell & Farnsworth (a San Francisco financial specialist), Westgate Group (a north-east US financial services specialist) and the Amrop teams in Australia and New Zealand. The firm also acquired PA Consulting's recruitment business to complement Futurestep.

Korn/Ferry has one of the strongest global brands, with good representation across each of the three main regions as well as in many industries. In terms of earnings it is one of the top two firms worldwide and in the United States. It is market leader in Asia and Latin America and has a growing presence in Europe, where it is highly regarded for consumer goods, health care and life sciences. Management assessment represents 10–15% of the total business. As in most global firms, the level of cross-border referrals and the overall teamwork of consultants across borders could be improved. However, its aggressive and pioneering push into other HR services is worth watching.

According to Korn/Ferry, its biggest growth opportunities will come from further development of global accounts; increased market share through strategic hiring and aggressive internal recruiting by its local offices; and expansion of multiproduct "integrated services" offerings (that is, adding to the various HR services it provides).

Sectors and specialists

All e-mail addresses follow the same format: initiallastname@kornferry.com (eg, gkrassnig@kornferry.com)

Europe	Sector	Consultant
Austria	Board	Gerhard Krassnig
	Consumer	
	Industrial	
	Technology	
	Financial services	Herbert Unterkoefler
	Health care	Christoph la Garde
Belgium	Automotive, industry	Jean-Marie van den Borre
	Consumer	
	Health care	
	Financial services	Erwin de Wolf
	Media, entertainment	Anne Deghilage
	Technology	Philippe van Cutsem

Bucharest	Consumer	Radu Furnica
	Financial services	
	Industrial	
	Health care	
	Technology	
Budapest	Consumer	Vilmos Szabo
	Financial services	
	Industrial	
	Health care	
	Technology	
Denmark	Automotive, industry	Dick Andbert
	Consumer	
	Energy, oil	
	Financial services	
	Health care	
	Media, entertainment	
	Professional services	
	Technology	
Finland	Consumer	Ralf Hermansson
	Financial services	Hannu Viitanen
	Industrial	
	Technology	
	Health care	Ralf Hermansson
France	Automotive, industry	Remy Bellanger
	Consumer	Didier Vuchot
	Financial services	Bertrand Richard
	Health care	Marine de Boucaut
	Media, entertainment	Kalya Tea
	Technology	Jean Grellet
Germany	Automotive, industry	Alexander von Berg
	Consumer	Christoph Kleinen
	Financial services	Gerald Söhlemann
	Health care	Ernst-Jorg Zehelein
	Technology	Christiane Sauer
Greece	Consumer	Katherina Diamantopoulos
	Financial services	
	Industrial	
	Health care	
	Technology	Julia Ehrenfeld Levi
Italy	Automotive, industry	Raimundo Nider

	Consumer	Maura Nobili
	Media, entertainment	
	Financial services	Alberto Amaglio
	Health care	Daniele de Luca
	Technology	Massimo Canovi
Netherlands	Automotive, industry	Frans Visscher
	Health care	
	Consumer	Robert van Werhoven
	Financial services	Jan Vet
	Media, entertainment	Robert van Werkhoven
	Technology	Jan-Bart Smits
Norway	Consumer	Simen Mordre
	Financial services	Torbjorn Gjelstad
	Industrial	Olav Ropstad
	Health care	
	Technology	
Spain	Automotive, industry	Carlos Alemany
	Consumer	Jose Alises
	Media, entertainment	
	Financial services	Carlos Defauce
	Health care	Iliana de Cardenas
	Technology	Carlos Alemany
Sweden	Automotive, industry	Ulf Bergstrom
	Consumer	Dick Andbert
	Financial services	Mats Carlsson
	Technology	Per Haeggstrom
Switzerland	Consumer	Cornelia Taenzler
	Financial services	Michael McFadden
	Health care	Ludger Schwinn
	Technology	Thierry de Preux
Russia	All sectors	Sergei Serdioukov
UK	Automotive, industry	David Gibbs
	Consumer	Chris van Someren
	Media, entertainment	
	Financial services	Isabelle Martin Hotimsky
	Health care	Peter Bassett
	Professional services	David Burton
	Technology	Lisa Behlmann
	Board	Mina Gouran

North America

Canada	Automotive, industry Energy, oil	Bob Sutton
	Consumer Media, entertainment	Jeff Rosin
	Financial services	Dov Zevy
	Health care	Jack Penaligon
	Professional services	Denise Tobin-McCarthy
	Technology	John Mealia
US	Automotive, industry	Scott Kingdom
	Consumer	Tierney Remick
	Energy, oil	John McKay
	Financial services	Parker Harrell
	Health care	Cheryl Buxton
	Media, entertainment	Bill Simon
	Professional services	Craig Dunlevie
	Technology	Richard Spitz

Latin America

	Consumer	Maria Elena Valdes
	Financial services	Rafael Gonzalez
	Automotive, industry	Eduardo Taylor
	Life sciences	Robert Wong
	Technology	Carlos Gonzalez

Asia & Australasia

Australia	Automotive, industry	Gary Reidy
	Consumer Health care Media, entertainment	Daniel Gauchat
	Energy, oil	Gary Reidy
	Financial services	Paul Rowe
	Professional services Technology	John Powell
China	Automotive, industry Energy, oil	C.K. Lai
	Consumer Media, entertainment	Lynn Ogden
	Financial services	Andrew Tsui
	Health care	Ling Li

	Professional services Technology	Alan Choi
Japan	Automotive, industry Energy, oil	Ken Koyama
	Consumer Media, entertainment	Sakie Fukushima
	Financial services	Kazumi Fujimura
	Health care	Teruo Seno
	Professional services Technology	Kaori Iwamoto
India	Automotive, industry Energy, oil Health care	Madhav Sharan
	Consumer Media, entertainment	Ketaki Gupte
	Financial services	Deepak Gupta
	Professional services Technology	Gita Dang

Middle East & Africa

Middle East	All sectors	Metin Mitchell
South Africa	All sectors	Brian Khumalo
Turkey	All sectors	Serif Kaynar

Heidrick & Struggles International

Senior management

Chairman and CEO . . . . .Thomas J. Friel
Regional managing partners . .Americas: Bonnie W. Gwin
           Europe, Middle East, Africa: Thomas J. Friel
           (acting)
           Asia Pacific: L. Kevin Kelly

Board of directors

Richard I. Beattie

Antonio Borges

John A. Fazio

Thomas J. Friel

Jill Kanin-Lovers

Robert E. Knowling Jr

Gerard R. Roche

Paul Unruh

Douglas C. Yearley

Headquarters

North America
233 S. Wacker Drive, Suite 7000
Chicago, IL 60606
US
Tel: +1 312 496 1000

Europe
3 Burlington Gardens
London W1S 3EP
UK
Tel: +44 20 7075 4000

Website

www.heidrick.com

Office locations

Europe	Amsterdam, Barcelona, Berlin, Brussels, Copenhagen, Dusseldorf, Frankfurt, Hamburg, Helsinki*, Istanbul*, Lisbon, London, Madrid, Milan, Munich (Residenzstrasse), Munich (Keplerstrasse), Paris, Rome, Stockholm, Vienna, Warsaw, Zurich
Americas	Atlanta, Bogota*, Boston, Buenos Aires, Caracas*, Chicago, Cleveland, Dallas, Denver, Greenwich, Houston, Lima*, Los Angeles, Menlo Park, Mexico City, Miami, New York (Park Avenue), New York (Wall Street), Philadelphia, San Francisco, Santiago, São Paulo, Toronto, Tysons Corner
Asia & Australasia	Beijing, Hong Kong, Melbourne, Mumbai, New Delhi, Seoul, Shanghai, Singapore, Sydney, Taipei, Tokyo
Middle East & Africa	Johannesburg*

*Affiliate office

Practice groups

Industry

Business and professional services	Industrial
Communications, networking and equipment providers	Life sciences
Consumer products	Media, entertainment, leisure and hospitality
Consumer technology	Private equity/venture capital
Financial services	Real estate and construction
Hardware, semiconductors and systems	Retail
	Software

Functional

Board of directors	Chief legal officer and legal services (CLO)
Chief financial officer (CFO)	
Chief human resources officer (CHRO)	Supply chain
Chief information officer (CIO)	

Regionally focused

Diversity services	Hospitals, systems and services
Education and non-profit	Managed care

Services offered

Executive search
Management audit and executive assessment
Executive coaching and professional development
Interim executive placement

Global performance data

Figures are for 2004, except industry sector and function which are for 2003

Net revenue	$375.4m
Number of partners	297[a]
Number of researchers	310
Net revenue per consultant	$1.26m
Number of offices worldwide	58
% change in net revenue 2003/04	18.1

a Includes consultants.

Global net revenue by industry sector (%)

Consumer	16
Education, non-profit	3
Financial services	28
Health care	9
Industrial	20
Professional services	9
Technology	15

Global net revenue by function (%)

CEO, president, board director	21
Chief financial officer	11
Chief information officer	4
Chief operating officer	4
Human resources	4
Legal	4
Other	52

Net revenue by geographic region (%)

North America	54
Europe	34
Asia & Australasia	8
Latin America	3

Comments

Heidrick & Struggles was founded in Chicago in 1953 by Gardner Heidrick & John Struggles. In 1957 the firm signed its first clients outside the midwest and in 1968 opened its first office overseas in London. Sector practices were launched in the United States in 1983 and in Europe in 1987. The firm began to build a presence in Asia with the opening of an office in Sydney in 1989 followed by Tokyo in 1991. Heidrick was the pioneer of the speciality practice group and established a world-class reputation, particularly in the technology and industrial sectors. It has always been at the forefront of its industry in terms of internet technology and online databases.

Heidrick & Struggles became a publicly owned company in 1999 and is traded on the NASDAQ stockmarket. In the same year the firm launched an internet-based company, Leaders on Line, but it decided to withdraw from this middle-management business and closed the operation in 2001.

The company has a strong global brand and is ranked number one in the world in revenue terms. Regionally it is strong too: it is ranked two in the United States, is one of the top five companies in Europe and is among the leading brands in Asia.

Acquisitions have included Mulder & Partner (the market leader in Germany) in 1997, Sullivan & Partners (a financial services specialist in New York) in 1999 and SHP Associates (a specialist in middle-management search in technology and financial services in the UK) in 2001. Since 2002 the firm also has had a joint venture with Lore International Institute, a specialist in assessment and coaching based in the United States.

Heidrick is strong in technology, not-for-profit, education, energy, financial services and consumer goods. In the UK it is also well respected in public-sector business. However, the firm suffered badly during the recent downturn, shedding 700 staff, and needs to rebuild some practice groups in Europe, such as life sciences and its non-executive/board practice. However, it suffered badly during the recent downturn, shedding 700 staff, and needs to rebuild some practice groups in Europe, such as life sciences and boards.

Biggest growth opportunities

According to the firm, the focus for growth will be searches and services for boards, CEOs and other senior executives and related "leadership" services. To achieve this, Heidrick is focusing on what it calls "target accounts", who have demonstrated the potential to become long-term partners. It is also restructuring its organisation to support these clients; formerly its structure was based primarily on geography and industries.

Biggest challenges

After the painful experiences of 2001–02, when it found its well-being was tied far more closely to the global economy than it had previously thought, Heidrick reduced costs and brought its expenditure under better control. It has gone through a series of restructurings to amalgamate separate firms in Europe and the Americas into one global organisation. Probably the biggest challenge for the firm is in developing ways to differentiate itself from the competition, which has become stronger.

Sectors and specialists

All e-mail addresses follow the same format: initiallastname@heidrick.com
(eg, flerno@heidrick.com)

Europe	Sector	Consultant
Belgium	Consumer	Filip Lerno
	Financial services	
Denmark	Automotive, industry	Ivan Henriques
	Consumer	Christen Dalum
	Financial services	Henrik Greisen
	Health care	Tobias Petri
	Professional services	
	Technology	
France	Consumer	Sylvie Maillot
	Media, entertainment	
	Health care	Solange Combe
	Professional services	Emeric Lepoutre
	Technology	Guy de Buttet
Germany	Consumer	Hans Dietlef Pries
	Energy, oil	Klaus Ader
	Financial services	Sabine Wehle
	Industry (generalist)	Reinhard Theil
	Insurance	Christoph Netta
	Media, entertainment	Peter Osthues
	Professional services	Clemens von Guggenberg
	Real estate	Werner Knips
	Technology	Mathias Hiebeler
		Michael Sorokin
		Wolfgang Walter
Italy	Automotive, industry	Leonardo Frezza
	Health care	
	Consumer	Giovanni Mantica
	Media, entertainment	
	Financial services	Maurizia Villa
Netherlands	Automotive, industry	Han van Halder
	Consumer	Ollo den Tex
	Health care	
	Media, entertainment	
	Professional services	
	Energy, oil	Daan de Roos

	Financial services	Per Insinger
	Technology	Jean Pierre Dubois
Spain	Automotive, industry	Michael Rosenberg
	Consumer	Luis Urbano
	Health care	Ignacio Bello
	Technology	Stefano Salvatore
Sweden	Automotive, industry	Bengt Lejsved
	Financial services	Monica Lagercrantz
	Health care	Thord Thorstensson
	Technology	Goran Rotzius
Switzerland	Consumer	Bernard S. Zen-Ruffiner
	Media, entertainment	Romeo Crameri
UK	Automotive, industry	John Spurling
	Consumer	Chris Long
	Consumer, retail	Fran Minogue
	Education, not-for-profit	Gill Lewis
	Energy, oil	Richard Emerton
	Financial services	Sonomara Jeffrey
	Interim management	David Peters
	Media, entertainment	Tim Hammett
	Professional services	Amanda Alexander
	Technology	Simon Buirski

North America

US	Professional services	Madeleine Pfau
	Technology	Jean Louis Alpyerie
		John Strackhouse
		Dora Vell
	IT, professional services	Bonnie Gwin
	Board	Joie Gregor
	CIOs	Jory Morino
		Kelvin Thompson

Asia & Australasia

Australia	Automotive, industry	Jim Hayman
	Consumer	David Pumphrey
	Professional services	
	Health care	Ron Graham
	Technology	Gerry Davis

China	Automotive, industry	Steven Gu
	Consumer	Vincent Swift
	Media, entertainment	
	Professional services	James Gathercole
	Technology	Kyung Yoon
Japan	Financial services	Kevin Kelly

Spencer Stuart

Senior management
CEO . . . . .David Daniel
Regional managers . . . . .United States: Kevin Connelly
Europe: Manuel Marquez
Asia: David Daniel
Latin America: Ignacio Marseillan

Board of directors

Rich Brennen

Jason Chaffer

Jim Citrin

Carlo Corsi

David Daniel

Henri de Pitray

Carolyn Eadie

Joe Kopsick

Rich Kurkowski

John Mumm

Tom Neff

Dayton Ogden (chairman)

Headquarters
401 N. Michigan Avenue
Suite 2600
Chicago, IL 60611
US
Tel: +1 312 822 0088

Website
www.spencerstuart.com

Office locations
Europe	Amsterdam, Barcelona, Brussels, Budapest, Frankfurt, Geneva, Leeds, London, Madrid, Manchester, Milan, Munich, Paris, Prague, Rome, Stockholm, Vienna, Warsaw, Zurich
Americas	Atlanta, Bogota, Boston, Buenos Aires, Chicago, Dallas, Houston, Irvine, Los Angeles, Mexico City, Miami, Minneapolis/St Paul, Montreal, New York, Philadelphia, San Francisco, San Mateo, Santiago, São Paulo, Stamford, Toronto, Washington DC
Asia & Australasia	Beijing, Hong Kong, Melbourne, Shanghai, Singapore, Sydney, Tokyo
Middle East & Africa	Johannesburg

Practice groups

Industry

Consumer goods and services	Industrial
Education, non-profit and public policy	Life sciences
Financial services	Technology, communications and media

Functional

Board services	Human resources
Diversity	Information officer
Financial officer	Legal search

Services offered

Board services
Executive assessment
Executive search (including advertised selection in certain markets)

Global performance data

Figures are for financial year ending September 2004; industry sector, function and geographic region are for 2003

Net revenue	$362.4m
Number of partners	292[a]
Number of researchers	197[b]
Net revenue per consultant	$1.24m
Number of offices worldwide	49
% change in net revenue 2003/04	18.2

a Includes consultants. b Excluding research assistants.

Global net revenue by industry sector (%)

Automotive, industrial	16
Consumer, retail	17
Energy, oil	7
Financial services	19
Foundations, not-for-profit	2
Pharmaceuticals, health care, biotechnology	14
Professional services, consulting, marketing & communications	7
Technology, communications & media	17
Other	1

Global net revenue by function (%)

Asset management	3
CEO, managing director, COO, general manager	29
Communications	1
Financial	14
IT, technology	4
Human resources	5
Legal	3
Marketing and sales	16
Non-executive directors, chairmen	10
Not-for-profit, education	1
Operations and production	5
Planning development	1
Professional services	2
Research and scientific	2
Other	5

Net revenue by geographic region (%)

North America	61
Europe, Africa, Middle East	30
Asia Pacific	7
Latin America	2

Comments

The firm was founded in Chicago in 1956 by Spencer Stuart. In 1974, after his retirement in 1973, it became an international partnership. It opened its first European office in Zurich in 1958 followed by one in London in 1961. The firm is privately and wholly owned by its consultants and is determined to remain so. As Manuel Marquez, managing director of Europe, explains:

> *Whereas other firms chose to go public, we elected to focus on quality and client service; to become the best, not the biggest firm; and to maintain a partnership not a corporate culture.*

Spencer Stuart has a strong global brand, with 49 offices in 25 countries, and in revenue terms is ranked in the top three worldwide, first in the United States and one of the top three firms in Europe. It also has an excellent reputation in Latin America and Asia and Australasia. The firm is especially known for its senior board and CEO practices – CEO searches have included Yahoo!, Tyco, Motorola and the New York Stock Exchange. Its global board services practice conducted more than 400 assignments in 2003. Advertised recruitment is conducted in just four countries: Australia, Italy, the Netherlands and the UK. This side of the business is integrated with the search business and uses the same consultants.

The firm has acquired several small businesses over the years but, in general, its strategy is to grow organically. Spencer Stuart has had a strategic alliance in Russia since 2001 with Ward Howell, with which it collaborates on a range of international and cross-border searches.

As the largest privately held executive search firm, Spencer Stuart boasts a strong partnership culture and claims that two-thirds of its assignments are for repeat clients. However, the United States and the UK account for 70% of Spencer Stuart's business, so there are growth opportunities in Continental Europe, Asia and Latin America.

The firm recognises the need to make sure that its consultants work across borders on multicountry assignments with the same dedication and professionalism they show to clients in their local markets, and feels it has made good progress on this, especially in Europe.

Marquez says:

> We expect to see boards and nominating committees take a greater role in executive appointments. They will seek more depth to the professional advice offered by executive search consultants and demand a higher level of specialisation, quality in the assessment of the candidates we present and rigour in the due diligence process. We believe this trend, now very evident in the US, will rapidly move to other regions of the world.

Sectors and specialists

All e-mail addresses follow the same format: initiallastname@ spencerstuart.com (eg, gwilhelm@spencerstuart.com)

Europe	Sector	Consultant
Austria	Automotive, industry Technology	Gerhard Resch-Fingerlos
	Boards	Gerd Wilhelm
	Consumer	
	Financial services	

	Energy, oil	Gerhard Oberhuber
		Gerd Wilhelm
	Health care	Gerhard Oberhuber
	Media, entertainment	Gerhard Resch-Fingerlos
		Gerd Wilhelm
	Professional services	Gerhard Resch-Fingerlos
		Gerhard Oberhuber
		Gerd Wilhelm
Belgium	Automotive, industry	Jean-Marie De Dobbelaere
	Professional services	
	Boards	Jean-Marie De Dobbelaere
	Technology	Henk Slabbinck
	Consumer	Henk Slabbinck
	Energy, oil	
	Media, entertainment	
	Financial services	Jean-Marie De Dobbelaere
		Henk Slabbinck
	Health care	Yannick Hecaen
Czech Republic	All sectors	Tibor Gedeon
		Karel Pobuda
France	Automotive, industry	Jean-Pierre Catu
		Henri de Pitray
	Boards	Henri de Pitray
	Consumer	Bruno-Luc Banton
		Danièle Beitz
		Henri de Pitray
		Xavier de Boissard
	Energy, oil	Peter Bogin
	Financial services	Dominique Potiron
	Health care	Yannick Hecaen
	Professional services	
	Technology	
	Media, entertainment	Bruno-Luc Banton
		Danièle Beitz
Germany	Automotive, industry	Reinhold Thiele
	Boards	Yvonne Beiertz
		Hartwig Knitter
		Willi Schoppen
	Consumer	Christine Stimpel
	Energy, oil	Hartwig Knitter

	Financial services	Yvonne Beiertz
	Health care	Christine Stimpel
	Media, entertainment	Otto Obermaier
	Professional services	Uwe Pavel
	Technology	Lutz Tilker
		Bruno Weidl
Hungary	All sectors	András Gábor
Italy	Automotive, industry	Simone Maggiani
	Boards	Luca Pacces
	Consumer	Mauro Capriata
	Energy, oil	Gabriele Ghini
	Financial services	Andrea Pecchio
	Health care	Barbara Virgilio
	Media, entertainment	Pierpaolo Morelli
	Professional services	
	Technology	Umberto Bussolati
Netherlands	Automotive, industry	Hans Becks
		Sandor Koster
		Manfred Mulder
	Boards	Pieter-Paul Peters
	Consumer	Yvonne Jung
		Maarten Tuininga
		Britt Van den Berg
	Energy, oil	Hans Becks
		Ger Scholtens
	Financial services	Sandor Koster
		Nico Schrijen
		Ger Scholtens
	Health care	Hans Becks
		Yvonne Yung
	Media, entertainment	Herman Krommendam
	Professional services	Hans Becks
		Martin Heijman
	Technology	Martin Heijman
		Herman Krommendam
		Manfred Mulder
Poland	All sectors	Urszula Szostek

Spain	Automotive, industry	Fernando Masiá
	Boards	Ignacio Gil-Casares
		Francisco Gasset
		Luis Ferrándiz
		Manuel Marquez
	Consumer	Francisco Gasset
	Energy, oil	Luis Ferrándiz
	Financial services	Ignacio Maza
		Salvador Palmada
	Health care	Jorge Barbat
	Media, entertainment	Pablo Bernad
		Fernando Masiá
	Professional services	Ignacio Gil-Casares
		Ignacio Maza
	Technology	Pablo Bernad
		Manuel Marquez
Sweden	Automotive, industry	Mats Ottosson
	Boards	Göran Westberg
	Consumer	Frans Benson
	Professional services	Frans Benson
	Energy, oil	Göran Westberg
	Financial services	Frans Benson
	Health care	Per Sanström
	Media, entertainment	Göran Westberg
	Technology	Per Sandström
Switzerland	Automotive, industry	Roger Rytz
	Boards	
	Technology	
	Consumer	François Clerc
	Energy, oil	
	Financial services	Maurice Zufferey
		Fredy Isler
	Health care	Phil LeGoff
	Media, entertainment	François Clerc
		Fredy Isler
		Roger Rytz
	Professional services	Fredy Isler
UK	Automotive, industry	Fergus Wilson

	Boards	Carolyn Eadie
		Anne Ferguson
		Jan Hall
		David Kimbell
		Stephen Patrick
	Consumer	Carole Fairfield
		Fleur Cowley
		Becky Falkingham
		Nick Green
		Johnathan Smith
		Edward Speed
	Energy, oil	Fergus Wilson
	Financial services	Phil Bainbridge
		Jason Chaffer
		Marc Eschauzier
		Simon Fenton
		Chris Hart
		David Juster
		Katherine Moos
		Peter Williamson
	Health care	Simon Russell
	Media, entertainment	Jan Hall
	Professional services	Carolyn Eadie
		Simon Russell
	Technology	Rob Wilder
		Tony Vardy
North America		
Canada	Automotive, industry	John Koopman
	Consumer	Roger Clarkson
	Energy, oil	Jerry Bliley
	Financial services	Andrew MacDougall
	Health care	Roger Clarkson
	Media, entertainment	Sharon Rudy
		Jeff Hauswirth
	Professional services	Carter Powis
	Technology	Jeff Hauswirth
	Boards	Andrew MacDougall
		Jerry Bliley
Mexico	Automotive, industry	Rafael Rojo

	Boards	Rafael Rojo
	Consumer	Javier Valle
	Energy, oil	
	Financial services	
	Media, entertainment	
	Professional services	
	Technology	
	Health care	Javier Valle
US	Automotive, industry	Bob Heidrick
	Consumer	Joe Kopsick
	Energy, oil	Richard Preng
		Bob Shields
	Financial services	Connie McCann
	Health care	Joe Boccuzi
	Media, entertainment	Jim Citrin
	Professional services	Randy Kelley
	Technology	Rich Brennen
	Boards	Julie Daum

Latin America

	Automotive, industry	Felipe Assumpcao
	Boards	Guilherme Dale
	Consumer	Alfonso Mujica
	Energy, oil	Fernando Matthei
	Financial services	Alejandro Etchart
	Health care	Rudolph Mayer-Singule
	Media, entertainment	Eliana Stigol
	Professional services	Fernando Carneiro
	Technology	Edgardo Lijtmaer

Asia & Australasia

Australia	Automotive, industry	David Small
		John Mumm
	Consumer	Mike Wheatley
		Kevin Jurd
	Energy, oil	David Small
		John Mumm
	Financial services	Kerri Burgess
		John Rees

	Health care	Liane Kemp
		Neil Martin
	Media, entertainment	Kevin Jurd
	Professional services	Michael Lamb
		Neil Martin
	Technology	Michael Lamb
		Susie Young
	Boards	John Mumm
		Michael Wheatley
Greater China	Automotive, industry	Peter Roberts
		Jwee San Tan
	Boards	Martin Tang
	Consumer	Peter Roberts
		Martin Tang
	Energy, oil	Jwee San Tan
	Financial services	Margaret Lee
	Professional services	
	Health care	Martin Tang
	Media, entertainment	Tim Hoffman
	Technology	
Japan	Automotive, industry	Joji Hara
		Shozo Yanagi
	Boards	Joji Hara
	Consumer	Joji Hara
		Sumio Saitoh
	Energy, oil	Soichi Goto
		Shozo Yanagi
	Financial services	Peter Rackowe
		Junichiro Tsuji
		Toshikazu Yabuno
	Health care	Soichi Goto
		Koichi Naruse
	Media, entertainment	Koichi Naruse
		Joji Hara
	Professional services	Soichi Goto
		Joji Hara
		Sunio Saitoh
	Technology	Joji Hara
		Hidekazu Kuraguchi

Middle East & Africa

South Africa	Automotive, industry Consumer	Rob Smith
	Boards	Mpho Seboni
	Energy, oil	Rob Smith
	Financial services	Marco Boni Mpho Seboni
	Health care	Chris van Melle Kamp
	Media, entertainment	Marco Boni
	Professional services	Mpho Seboni Chris van Melle Kamp
	Technology	Mpho Seboni

Egon Zehnder International

Senior management

Executive chairman . . . . .A. Daniel Meiland (New York)
CEO .John J. Grumbar (London)

Headquarters

North America
Egon Zehnder International
350 Park Avenue, 8th Floor
New York, NY 10022
US
Tel: +1 212 519 6000

Europe
Dr Egon Zehnder & Partner AG
Toblerstrasse 80
8044 Zurich
Switzerland
Tel: +41 1 267 6969

Website

www.egonzehnder.com

Office locations

Europe	Amsterdam, Athens, Barcelona, Berlin, Brussels, Budapest, Copenhagen, Dusseldorf, Frankfurt, Geneva, Hamburg, Helsinki, Istanbul, Lisbon, London, Luxembourg, Lyon, Madrid, Milan, Moscow, Munich, Paris, Prague, Rome, Stuttgart, Vienna, Warsaw, Zurich
Americas	Atlanta, Bogota, Boston, Buenos Aires, Chicago, Dallas, Los Angeles, Mexico City, Miami, Montreal, New York, Palo Alto, Rio de Janeiro, San Francisco, Santiago, São Paulo, Toronto
Asia & Australasia	Hong Kong, Jakarta, Kuala Lumpur, Melbourne, Mumbai, New Delhi, Shanghai, Seoul, Singapore, Sydney, Tokyo
Middle East & Africa	Dubai, Jeddah, Tel Aviv

Practice groups

Boards and non-executive directors
Consumer
Financial services
Foundations and not-for-profit
Industrial

Life sciences
Private capital
Services
Technology and telecoms

Services offered
Executive search
Management audit
Board appointments and reviews

Global performance data
Figures are for 2004

Net revenue	$335.7m
Number of partners	290
Number of researchers	n/a
Net revenue per consultant	$1.18m
Number of offices worldwide	59
% change in net revenue 2003/04	23.5

Comments
Egon Zehnder International was the first executive search firm to be founded outside the United States. It was set up in Zurich in 1964 by Egon Zehnder, who had previously worked at Spencer Stuart, for whom he opened several European offices. It is now a private firm owned by its consultants, each of whom owns an equal share. With offices in 37 countries, it has a strong global brand, being rated number one in Europe by industry observers, and is one of the leading firms in Asia and Latin America, where it has maintained a presence despite difficult economic times. It is also building its presence in the Middle East (see Office locations opposite; the Istanbul office also serves this region).

The firm operates as a single profit centre with a one-firm compensation system ("one world, one firm") whereby all consultants are remunerated on the basis of the firm's (not the individual's) profits. It also charges on a fixed-fee basis (rather than a percentage of salary) agreed in advance of the work and according to the significance, difficulty and scope of the search.

All this, the firm claims, ensures that its clients' interests come first. A single profit centre removes potential competition between offices, which can happen in other firms, and a one-firm compensation system motivates consultants to work across borders for clients and to put as much effort into assisting a partner in another market on a multicountry search as they would into one in their own local market. Egon Zehnder claims to have pioneered the fixed-fee policy, which, it says, means consultants are less likely to be biased when recommending candidates because there is no incentive for them to favour those with higher salaries or to exclude internal candidates. This approach, claims the firm, also means that the fee charged to the client is based on a more accurate estimate of the cost and complexity of the assignment.

Egon Zehnder is especially strong and highly regarded in Europe, Latin America and Asia, and although it has only 11 offices in the United States, it is among the top six firms in terms of revenue, and its cross-border work is highly regarded. It also has an excellent reputation for training and development of its consultant team and claims to have one of the highest retention rates in the business.

Management appraisal is a growing sector which now accounts for 20% of Egon Zehnder's global revenue. All the firm's consultants are trained in management appraisal techniques. Board evaluation and board review led by Christopher Thomas in Paris are also growth areas. The firm believes that Asia and the United States will offer the biggest opportunities and challenges in the coming years.

Sectors and specialists

All e-mail addresses follow the same format: firstname.lastname@ezi.net (eg, boudewijn.arts@ezi.net)

Europe	Sector	Consultant
Belgium	Automotive, industry	Boudewijn Arts
	Consumer	Karsten M. De Clerck
	Energy, oil	Pierre Cattoir
	Financial services	Guy Detrilles
	Health care	Nicolas Hollanders
	Media, entertainment	Karel Baert
	Professional services	Joost Maes
	Technology	Pierre Cattoir
Denmark	Automotive, industry	Lars Bo Jorgensen
	Financial services	
	Technology	
	Consumer	Thomas Wamberg
	Energy, oil	Henrik Aagaard
	Health care	
	Media, entertainment	Claus Colliander
	Professional services	
France	Automotive, industry	Didier Duez
	Energy, oil	
	Consumer	Lisa Barlow
	Financial services	Daniel Tournier

	Health care	Philippe Pinlon
	Technology	Pierre Mogenet
Germany	Automotive, industry	Jorg Ritter
	Consumer	Stephan Buchner
	Energy, oil	Nicolas von Rosty
	Financial services	Volker Christians
	Health care	Johannes von Schmettow
	Media, entertainment	Stephan Buchner
	Professional services	Karin Siegle
	Technology	Michael Ensser
Italy	Automotive, industry	Francesco Queirolo
	Consumer	Claudio Ceper
	Energy, oil	Stefano Scarpa
	Financial services	Alessandro di Fusco
	Health care	Paolo Veneziani
	Professional services	Serenella Sala
	Technology	
Netherlands	Automotive, industry	Edwin Smelt
	Energy, oil	
	Consumer	Johan Brand
	Financial services	Hans Horn
	Health care	Sikko Onnes
	Media, entertainment	Albert Laverge
	Professional services	Annekee Hulshoff Pol
	Technology	David Majtlis
Norway	Automotive, industry	Morten Tveit
	Consumer	Fred O. Jacobsen
	Energy, oil	
	Financial services	Magnus Sandkvist
	Health care	Stefan Nilsson
	Media, entertainment	Morten Tveit
Spain	Automotive, industry	Juan Torras
	Consumer	Pilar Giron
	Financial services	Ignacio Gasset
	Health care	Ramon Reyes
	Technology	Alvaro Arias Echeverria
Sweden	Automotive, industry	Torgny Segerberg
	Consumer	Stefan Nilsson
	Energy, oil	Björn Malmgren
	Financial services	Magnus Sandkvist

	Health care	Stefan Nilsson
	Media, entertainment	Lanny Nilsson
	Professional services	Carl Edenhammar
	Technology	Peter Berntsson
Switzerland	Automotive, industry	Philippe Hertig
	Energy, oil	
	Consumer	Thomas Allgauer
	Financial services	Clemens Hoegl
	Health care	Chris Muggli
	Media, entertainment	Beat Geissler
	Technology	
	Professional services	Peter Baltensperger
UK	Automotive, industry	Andrew Roscoe
	Consumer	Peggy Cornwell
	Energy, oil	David Kidd
	Financial services	Andrew Lowenthal
	Health care	Laurence Monnery
	Media, entertainment	Andrew Gilchrist
	Professional services	Ashley Summerfeld
	Technology	Tim Cook

North America

Canada	Automotive, industry	Jon Martin
	Consumer	David Harris
		Tom Long
	Energy, oil	Jon Martin
	Financial services	Jan Stewart
	Health care	Pamela Warren
	Media, entertainment	Valerie Spriet
	Professional services	Tom Long
	Technology	Rashid Wasti
US	Automotive, industry	Karl Alleman
	Consumer	Justus O'Brien
	Financial services	Alan Hilliker
	Health care	Jeff Dodson
	Professional services	Keith Meyer
	Technology	Ross Brown

Latin America

Argentina	Consumer	Juan Peborg
	Financial services	Jorge Steverlinck
	Health care	
	Technology	Marcelo Grimoldi
Brazil	Automotive, industry	Christian Spremberg
	Consumer	Luis Giolo
	Health care	
	Media, entertainment	
	Energy, oil	Edilson Camara
	Financial services	Joao Aquino de Souza
	Professional services	Sam Osmo
	Technology	
Chile	Consumer	Jose Garreaud
Mexico	Consumer	Antonio Puron
	Technology	
	Health care	Ricardo Weihman

Asia & Australasia

Australia	Automotive, industry	Kokkong Cham
	Financial services	Kokkong Cham
	Consumer	Jane Allen
	Media, entertainment	
	Energy, oil	Ashley Stephenson
	Health care	Chris Figgis
	Professional services	Nikki Dawson
	Technology	Neil Waters
China	Automotive, industry	Benjamin Zhai
	Consumer	Hillary Wood Chan
	Energy, oil	Xuecheng Zheng
	Financial services	Jackie Wong
	Health care	Walter Hungerbuhler
	Media, entertainment	Siddique Salleh
	Professional services	Jackie Wong
	Technology	Dennis Ku
Japan	Automotive, industry	Yoshiaki Obata
	Consumer	Mika Masuyama
	Financial services	Nobuo Sato
	Health care	Takahiro Oishi
	Professional services	Hideaki Tsukuda

	Technology	Isao Sakai
India	Automotive, industry	Anjali Bansal
		Govind Iyer
	Consumer	Sonny Iqbal
	Media, entertainment	
	Professional services	
	Energy, oil	Sanjiv Sachar
	Health care	
	Financial services	Namrita Jhangiani
		Sanjiv Sachar
	Technology	Rajeev Vasudeva
		Govind Iyer

Middle East & Africa

UAE	All sectors	Haider Shaif (Dubai)

Russell Reynolds Associates

Senior management

Chairman, president & CEO . . . . . .Hobson Brown Jr
Head of the Americas . . . . .P. Clarke Murphy
Head of Europe and Asia Pacific . . .Matthew Wright
Sector co-leaders . . . . .John Archer, Rae Sedel

Board of directors

Robert P. Bauman	Frederick W. Gluck
John C. Beck	Landon Hilliard
Hobson Brown Jr	Judith Richards Hope
Jonathan J. Bush	Claude L. Janssen
Philip Caldwell	Dennis G. Little
Kevin Carton	Robert G. Stone Jr

Headquarters

200 Park Avenue, Suite 2300
New York, NY 10166
US
Tel: +1 212 351 2000

Website

www.russellreynolds.com

Office locations

Europe	Amsterdam, Brussels, Copenhagen, Frankfurt, Hamburg, London, Madrid, Milan, Munich, Paris, Stockholm, Warsaw
Americas	Atlanta, Boston, Chicago, Dallas, Houston, Los Angeles, Menlo Park, Mexico City, Minneapolis/St Paul, New York, San Francisco, São Paulo, Toronto, Washington DC
Asia & Australasia	Hong Kong, Melbourne, Shanghai, Singapore, Sydney, Tokyo

Practice groups

CEO and board services	Health care
Consumer markets	Industrial and natural resources
Corporate officers	Not-for-profit
Financial services	Technology

Services offered

Executive search	Executive assessment
Management audit	Diversity consulting

Global performance data

Figures are for 2004

Net revenue	$268m[a]
Number of partners	133
Number of researchers	n/a
Net revenue per consultant	$1.12m
Number of offices worldwide	32
% change in net revenue 2003/04	33

a November 2004 estimate.

Global net revenue by industry sector (%)

Consumer	15
Financial services	28
Health care	10
Industrial, natural resources	22
Technology	25

Net revenue by geographic region (%)

Americas	50
Europe, Middle East & Africa	41
Asia & Australasia	9

Comments

The firm was founded in 1969 by Russell Reynolds in New York and soon after expanded to Chicago, London and Paris. It is a private firm wholly owned by its directors and has a strong global brand with a "one-firm" culture, preferring to grow organically rather than by acquisition. In revenue terms, Russell Reynolds is ranked in the top four in the United States and in the top three in Europe, and it is increasing its presence in Asia.

It has traditionally been a market leader in financial services, although it has diversified its portfolio and is now also well respected in technology and telecoms, consumer and life sciences. Indeed, its technology practice is now equal in size to its financial services practice and is ranked number one by market share in the UK. Interestingly, Russell Reynolds's CEO and board services practice doubled in size in just three years between 2001 and 2004. The firm offers just one non-search service in the form of management assessment, which covers succession planning, merger and acquisition and private equity as well as board and executive team assessments. Russell Reynolds hopes to grow this business to 10–15% of its total revenue. The firm has an excellent reputation for training and developing its consultants.

The firm's growth in establishing offices worldwide has been modest, compared with the other four largest firms, but it claims that its goal has not been to be the largest firm but rather to produce work of the highest quality. Its revenue per consultant is often one of the highest in the industry, which indicates that it is certainly working at the highest level of executive search.

Russell Reynolds sees future growth opportunities across the board as economies rebound, but more specifically in health care, professional and business services, board and corporate officers, and management assessment.

Sectors and specialists

All e-mail addresses follow the same format: initiallastname@ russellreynolds.com (eg, fmarichal@russellreynolds.com)

Europe	Sector	Consultant
Belgium	Automotive, industry	Yves de Poucques
	Consumer Media, entertainment	Florence Marichal
	Energy, oil	Yves de Poucques
	Financial services	Jean van den Eynde Pascale Simon
	Health care Professional services	Yves de Poucques
	Technology	Sigrid Marz Daniela Krug
	Other	Jean van den Eynde (Europe legal practice leader)

Denmark	Automotive, industry Consumer Energy, oil Media, entertainment Health care	Jens Howitz
	Financial services Professional services	Steen Ernland
	Technology	Peter Gramkov
France	Automotive, industry	Christophe Tellier Carl Azar
	Consumer	Henry de Montebello Florence Ferraton
	Energy, oil	Christophe Tellier
	Financial services	Brigitte Lemercier Sonia de Demandolx Paul Jaeger Nicolas Manset
	Health care	Olivier Blin Emmanuelle Pichavant
	Media, entertainment	Henry de Montebello Florence Ferraton
	Professional services	Henry de Montebello Paul Jaeger Caroline Apffel
	Technology	Caroline Apffel Ahmad Hassan
Germany	Automotive, industry	Walter Friederichs Boris Jary (both Frankfurt)
	Consumer	Ulrike Rondas Ulrike Wieduwilt (both Hamburg)
	Energy, oil	Bernd Spies (Hamburg)
	Financial services	Matthias Scheiff Mark Unger (both Frankfurt)
	Health care	Ulrich Thess (Munich)
	Media, entertainment	Ulrike Wieduwilt (Hamburg)

	Professional services	Hazel Blaim (Hamburg)
	Technology	Thomas Becker (Frankfurt) Michael Oberwegner (Munich) Werner Penk (Hamburg)
Italy	Automotive, industry Energy, oil Technology	Alessandro Rovis
	Consumer	Beatrice Ballini Paola Calderini Mario Ceretti Massimo Picca
	Financial services	Alberto Gavazzi
	Health care	Mario Ceretti Massimo Picca
	Media, entertainment	Mario Ceretti Paola Calderini
	Professional services	Paola Calderini
Netherlands	Automotive, industry	Harm van Esch Hans Reus
	Consumer Energy, oil Media, entertainment	Harm van Esch
	Financial services	Rene de Zwaan
	Health care	Jacques Bouwens Taco van der Feltz
	Professional services	Hans Reus
	Technology	Harm van Esch Hans Reus
Poland	Automotive, industry	Katarzyna Bienkowska
	Consumer Financial services Professional services Technology	Dorota Czarnota
	Energy, oil Health care Media, entertainment	Katarzyna Bienkowska
Spain	Automotive, industry Consumer Media, entertainment	Javier Anitua Pedro Goenaga

	Energy, oil	Javier Anitua
		Ramon Gomez de Olea
	Financial services	Pedro Goenaga
	Health care	Jose Manuel Lopez
	Professional services	Jose Manuel Lopez
	Technology	Ramon Gomez de Olea
		Jose Manuel Lopez
Sweden	Automotive, industry	Anders Engman
	Consumer	Thord Thorstensson
	Health care	
	Media, entertainment	
	Energy, oil	Anders Engman
	Financial services	Monica Lagercrantz
	Professional services	
	Technology	Anders Engman
UK	Automotive, industry	Luke Meynell
		John Morris
		David Shellard
		Alan Winton
	Consumer	Peter Evans
	Energy, oil	Mat Green
	Financial services	Simon Hearn
		Emmanuelle Arthur
		Symon Elliott
		Lucia Ferreira
		James Hickman
		Dee Symons
	Health care	John Morris
		Pippa Shimmin
	Media, entertainment	Rosemary Collins
	Professional services	Adam Hale
		David Shellard
	Technology	Rae Sedel
		Kai Hammerich
		Adam Hale
		David Mills

North America

Canada	Financial services	Paul Cantor
		Shawn Cooper
	Professional services Technology	Paul Hudson
US	Automotive, industry	Robert Gariano (Chicago)
		Clarke Havener (Washington DC)
		William Henderson (New York)
		Richard Pierce (Chicago)
	Consumer	Joseph Bailey III (New York)
		Jim Carpenter (New York)
		Bobbie Lenga-Gutman (Chicago)
		Susanne Lyons (San Francisco)
		Brad McLane (Chicago)
		Kathryn Mitchell (Minn/St Paul)
	Energy, oil	John Freud (Houston)
		Lawrence Klock (Chicago)
		Don Lieb (Dallas)
		Steve Raben (Houston)
	Financial services	Sophie Ayres (New York)
		Nick Hurd (Boston)
		Rich Perkey (Atlanta)
		John Rogan (New York)
	Healthcare	John Archer (New York)
		Jay Kizer (Dallas)
	Media, entertainment	Joseph Bailey (New York)
		Jana Rich (San Francisco)
	Professional services	Peter Drummond-Hay (New York)
		Beth Olesky (New York, legal)
		Paul Zellner (Chicago)
	Technology	Charley Geoly (Menlo Park)
		Louise Goss-Custard (New York)
		Jana Rich (San Francisco)
		Tuck Rickards (Boston)

Latin America

Brazil	Automotive, industry Energy, oil Professional services	Jacques Sarfatti
	Consumer	Ricardo Rocco Fatima Zorzato
	Financial services	Dolph Johnson Fatima Zorzato
	Health care	Fabiana Bezerra Riccardo Rocco
	Media, entertainment	Riccardo Rocco Fatima Zorzato
	Technology	Antonio Mendonca Jacques Sarfatti Fatima Zorzato
Mexico	Automotive, industry	Eugenio Riquelme Rafael Yturbe
	Consumer Health care Media, entertainment Technology	Rafael Yturbe
	Energy, oil Financial services	Eugenio Riquelme

Asia & Australasia

Australia	Automotive, industry Energy, oil	Antony Beaumont (Melbourne)
	Consumer Media, entertainment	Heidi Mason (Sydney)
	Financial services	Lynn Anderson Heidi Mason (both Sydney)
	Professional services Technology	Graham Willis (Sydney)
China	Automotive, industry, Energy, oil	Peter Ng Gerald Lee David Nagy Kenneth Xu
	Consumer	Raymond Tang Cyril Chong Kenneth Xu

	Financial services	David Ng
		Jeremy Cheuk
		Raymond Tang
		May Tung
	Health care	Cyril Chong
		David Nagy
		Raymond Tang
	Media, entertainment	Cyril Chong
	Professional services	David Ng
	Technology	Paul Chau
		David Ng
Japan	Consumer	Gregg Greer
		Chihiro Tawara
	Financial services	Hirohide Fujii
		Yukihiro Koshiishi
		Samir Kothari
		Yuhiko Yasunaga
	Health care	Gregg Greer
	Media, entertainment	Chihiro Tawara
	Professional services	Yuko Yasuda
		Gregg Greer
		Toshiro Shimizu
	Technology	Masaaki Kaburagi
		Toshiro Shimizu
		Yuko Yasuda
Singapore	Automotive, industry	Patrick Fang
	Consumer	Mark Lam
	Energy, oil	Mark Lam
	Health care	Kathryn Yap
	Financial services	Choon Soo Chew
		Samir Kothari
	Media, entertainment	Kathryn Yap
	Professional services	Patrick Fang
	Technology	Mark Lam
		Kathryn Yap

Ray & Berndtson

Senior management
Co-chairmen . . . . .Roger Bekius (Netherlands)
Richard Boggis-Rolfe (UK)

Board of directors
Roger Bekius
Richard Boggis-Rolfe
Hakan Ekstrom
Ian Knop
Carl Lovas

Winston Pegler
David Peters
Kajus Rottok
Bill Weed

Headquarters
North America
Ray & Berndtson
405 Lexington Avenue, 26th Floor
New York, NY 10174
US
Tel: +1 212 9076501

Europe
Odgers Ray & Berndtson
11 Hanover Square
London W1S 1JJ
UK
Tel: +44 20 7529 1111

Websites
www.rayberndtson.com
www.odgers.com

Office locations
(Some cities have more than one office)

Europe	Amsterdam, Barcelona, Birmingham, Brussels, Budapest, Copenhagen, Frankfurt, Glasgow, Hamburg, Helsinki, Istanbul, Leeds, Lisbon, London, Madrid, Manchester, Milan, Moscow, Munich, Oslo, Paris, Prague, Stockholm, Vienna, Warsaw, Zurich
Americas	Atlanta, Buenos Aires, Calgary, Chicago, Halifax, Houston, Los Angeles, Mexico City, Montreal, New York, Ottawa, St John's, Santiago, São Paulo, Toronto, Vancouver
Asia & Australasia	Bangalore, Mumbai, Singapore, Sydney, Tokyo
Middle East & Africa	Cape Town, Dubai

Practice groups

Industry

Automotive
Business and professional services
Consumer products and services
E-business
Education and not-for-profit
Energy and utilities

Financial services
Health care and life sciences
Industrial products and services
Media
Technology

Functional

Board services
Chief financial officer
Chief information officer,
 chief technology officer

Human resources officer

Services offered

Executive search
Board of directors recruiting
Interim management

Leadership assessment
Succession planning

Global performance data

Figures are for 2003 unless stated otherwise

Net revenue	$147.4m[a]
Number of partners	300[b]
Number of researchers	200[c]
Net revenue per consultant	$491,333[a]
Number of offices worldwide	51
% change in net revenue 2003/04	16.8

a 2004. b Includes consultants. c Includes associates.

Global net revenue by industry sector (%)

Consumer products	2
Building, construction	3
Energy, utilities, agriculture, mining, forestry	2
Financial services	13
High-tech communication	8
Health care, chemical products	8
Industrial products	10
Professional services	5
Retail	11
Other	38

Global net revenue by function (%)

Finance and administration	12
General management	34
IT	2
Human resources	7
Marketing and sales	10
Manufacturing and engineering	1
Research and development	2
Other	32

Net revenue by geographic region (%)

Europe, Africa & Middle East	78
Americas	18
Asia & Australasia	4

Comments

Ray & Berndtson was founded in 1965 and is a partnership of interdependent firms. Its decentralised structure allows partner firms in each territory to retain financial independence and to manage themselves with a high degree of autonomy. The Ray & Berndtson partnership is built on two pillars: Berndtson, a long-established leading European group, joined forces in the 1990s with Paul R. Ray, a leading brand with over 30 years' experience in the United States. The European and American basis of the business was strengthened with the addition of partners in Asia and Latin America in the 1980s. The firm opened offices in the Middle East (Dubai) and South Africa in 2002 as well as additional offices in Canada, such as Calgary.

In 2000, Ray & Berndtson UK, part of the global firm, came together with Odgers in the UK. Odgers was founded in 1970 by Ian Odgers, who had built a respected generalist boutique firm in the UK. Odgers Ray & Berndtson also acquired The Berwick Group, a financial services specialist in 2001. Ray & Berndtson is the global name used for international work. Odgers as a prefix is used only in the UK, as, for example, is Profile – Profile Ray & Berndtson – in Australia. These prefixes apply to local markets and are the names of the firms that linked up with Ray & Berndtson.

Ray & Berndtson's structural model is unique and has helped it to become one of the leading firms in Europe and number six worldwide in terms of revenue. The group is well regarded for its work in chairman and main board appointments for quoted and private businesses, and government, health, education and other not-for-profit organisations.

Recent mandates in the UK to search for chairmen at the BBC, Royal Mail and the Wellcome Trust, as well as a mix of FTSE 1000, FTSE 250 and smaller-company chairmen and non-executive directors, demonstrate its range and level. Odgers Ray & Berndtson is a market leader in government and not-for-profit work and also has a long-standing reputation for handling top CFO and other finance searches.

The minimum fee is $50,000 in most markets and higher in several. With no external shareholders and no large corporate headquarters to divert funds, Ray & Berndtson says that "the focus is on serving clients, not on external bureaucracy and investors".

The group wants to strengthen its presence in the United States where the bulk of Ray & Berndtson (excluding the name) was acquired by A.T. Kearney, leaving an office in New York and a number of associates elsewhere. It also has no presence in Hong Kong or elsewhere in China, although plans are afoot to address this.

Sectors and specialists

E-mail address format varies.

Europe	Sector	Name
Austria	Energy	Joachim Zyla
	Eastern Europe	
	Financial services	
Belgium	Consumer	Baldwin Klep
	Financial services	Alain de Borchgrave
	Industry	Dominique Collet
		Jean-Charles Uyttenhove
	Logistics, automotive	Bernard Tobin
	Technology	Francis Vaningelgem
France	Consumer	Françoise de Metz-Noblat
	Financial services	Yves Boissonnat
		Gaëlde Roquefeuil
	Industry	Frédérique Moreau
	Technology	Xavier Alix
Germany	Automotive	Ralph Göller
	Consumer	Dirk Friederich
	Energy	Dieter Stein
		Jürgen van Zwoll
	Energy	Klaus Hansen
	Logistics	

	Financial services	Christine Kuhl
		Dirk Lindemann
		Kajus Rottok
	Health care	Hubert Lindenblatt
	Logistics	Alexander Zimmermann
	Professional services	Jörg Kasten
	Technology	Herbert Bechtel
Italy	Industry	Eduardo Salvia
Netherlands	Consumer	Michaël Mellink
	Health care	
	Energy	Patricia Flipsen
	Financial services	Roger Bekius
	Industry	
	Professional services	
	Logistics	Monique Gerrits
Spain	Financial services	Luis José Murillo
	Technology	
	Industry	José Medina
	Professional services	
Sweden	Financial services	Hakan Ekström
	Professional services	
	Technology	
	Financial services	Anders Gudmarsson
Switzerland	Financial services	Ulrich Fehlmann
	Consumer	Max Schnopp
	Industry	
UK		
Birmingham	Automotive, industry	Simon North
		Peter Wittaker
	Industry	Oliver Howl
Glasgow	Financial services	Ian MacLeod
	Industry	Neville Washington
Leeds	Business, professional services	Jeff Morris
London	Board	Richard Boggis-Rolfe
		Virginia Bottomley
		Will Dawkins
	Business, professional services	Aine Hurley
		Alan Mumby
	Technology	Anna Ponton

	Consumer, retail	Sue Shipley
		Laurence Vallaeys
	Corporate communications	Victoria Provis
	Education	Diana Ellis
	Financial services	John Holmes
		Simon Mee
	Industry	William Burdett
		Bob Reynolds
	Not-for-profit	Frances Bell
		Nicky Oppenheimer
		Chris Stanford
Manchester	Industry	Mike Spurr
	Pharmaceuticals	

North America
Canada

Calgary	Energy	Kevin Hall
Montreal	Health care	Bernard Labrecque
	Technology	
Toronto	Industry	Carl Lovas
	Technology	Sue Banting

US

New York	Consumer	Tom Rosenwald
	Health care	Brian Kelley
	Media, entertainment	Tracy O'Such

Latin America

Brazil	Consumer	Francisco Britto
		Luiz Wever
	Energy	Uwe Laux
	Professional services	Winston Pegler

Asia & Australasia

India	Consumer	Mario Lobo
	Health care	
	Financial services	Clarence Lobo
	Technology	
Singapore	Financial services	Christopher See

The Amrop Hever Group

Senior management

Chairman . . . . Luis Conde (Barcelona)
Vice-chairmen . . . . Americas: Luis Carlos Cabrera
Asia Pacific: Tan Soo Jin
Europe, Middle East and Africa: Ulrich Dade
Executive director: Gerard J. Nauwelaerts

Board of directors

Stephen Bampfylde   Atul Kumar
Luis Carlos Cabrera   Addy Lee
Luis Conde   Svein Ruud
Ulrich Dade   Jacques Schoonbrood
George Enns   Tan Soo Jin
Hideaki Furuta

Headquarters

The Amrop Hever Group
Worldwide Secretariat
Avenue Louise 475 – Box 13
1050 Brussels
Belgium
Tel: +32 2 643 6000

Website

www.amrophever.com

Office locations

(Some cities have more than one office)
Europe   Amsterdam, Antwerp, Athens, Barcelona, Berlin,
Bratislava, Brussels, Bucharest, Budapest,
Copenhagen, Dresden, Dublin, Dusseldorf, Frankfurt,
Geneva, Gothenburg, Hamburg, Helsinki, Istanbul,
Lisbon, London, Lugano, Lyon, Madrid, Malmo, Milan,
Moscow, Munich, Oslo, Paris, Prague, Riga, Rome,
Sofia, Stockholm, Tallinn, Thessaloniki, Warsaw,
Vienna, Vilnius, Zurich

Americas	Bogota, Buenos Aires, Caracas, Chicago, Detroit, Guayaquil, Lima, Mexico City, Miami, Monterrey, New York, Quito, Santiago, São Paulo, Toronto
Asia & Australasia	Bangkok, Chennai, Hong Kong, Jakarta, Kuala Lumpur, Manila, Melbourne, Mumbai, New Delhi, Seoul, Shanghai, Singapore, Sydney, Tokyo, Wellington
Middle East & Africa	Beirut, Dubai, Johannesburg

Practice groups

Automotive and industrial	Health care and life sciences
Board appointments	IT and telecommunications
Consumer goods and retail	Management audit
Family business	Media
Financial services	Non-profit and public sector

Services offered

Executive coaching	Management audit
Executive search	

Global performance data

Figures are for 2004, except geographic regions which are for 2003

Net revenue	$135.3m
Number of partners	264[a]
Number of researchers	217
Net revenue per consultant	$512,500
Number of offices worldwide	79
% change in net revenue 2003/04	20.3

a Includes consultants.

Net revenue by geographic region (%)

Europe, Africa and Middle East	65
Asia and Australasia	16
North America	13
Latin America	6

Comments

The Amrop Hever Group was formed in 2000 when Amrop International and the Hever Group merged. Hever's presence in English-speaking markets was matched by Amrop's strength in Asia. Both had

European practices that merged well. The group operates as a semi-integrated network organised under an economic interest group which is incorporated under French law (a legal system enabling international co-operation of independent companies with a common business purpose). The legal entity is not a listed company but owns the group's registered trademarks. At present the group consists of 59 independent firms in five continents and has the largest geographical coverage of all the search firms.

Amrop Hever claims to combine entrepreneurial drive with in-depth local market knowledge and operates under a dual-branding policy, which means that in some markets the firm is principally known by its local name (for example, Rossignol Todd & Associés in France, D&G in Italy, Dr Besmer Consulting in Switzerland). Some of its firms are extremely well regarded in their markets: Saxton Bampfylde in the UK, Seeliger y Conde in Spain, PMC in Brazil, Cordiner King in Australia, Delta Amrop Hever in Germany and other Amrop Hever firms in India, Singapore, Russia, Austria and Scandinavia.

Although the group has global and listed blue-chip companies as clients, it also has a respected portfolio of family businesses throughout the world with a dedicated practice group under the direction of Luis Conde in Spain and Luis Cabrera in Brazil.

The group survived the worst recessionary years (2002–03) in the search industry with a global turnover loss of only 10%. For 2005 it projects annual turnover of around €128m ($158m).

Amrop Hever wants to build up its presence in the United States and get its brand name well established around the world. (In early 2005 Battalia Winston, ranked in the top 15 in the United States, joined the group.) It is well positioned in the fast-developing central and east European markets. An interesting feature is its global board of directors, composed of ten different nationalities in a three-year rotation system.

The group believes that continued pressure on fees and speed of delivery will be among the most serious challenges facing search firms, as well as increasing competition from contingency billing companies.

Sectors and specialists

E-mail address format varies.

Europe	Sector	Consultant
Belgium	Automotive, industry	Pieter Rens
	Consumer	Benoit Lison
	Energy, oil	Marc Daelemans
	Technology	
	Financial services	Tanguy Van Reeth
	Health care	
	Media, entertainment	Benoit Lison
	Professional services	Pieter Rens
Denmark	Automotive, industry	Kaj Taidal
	Consumer	Finn Krogh Rants
	Energy, oil	
	Financial services	Frank Halborg
	Health care	Eskil Westh
	Media, entertainment	Niels Bentzen
	Professional services	Niels Bentzen
		Finn Krogh Rants
	Technology	Niels Bentzen
		Eskil Westh
France (Lyon)	Automotive, industry	Jacques Petit
	Consumer	
	Energy, oil	
	Health care	
France (Paris)	Automotive, industry	Béatrice Folléa
	Consumer	Sylvain Pène
	Energy, oil	Béatrice Folléa
		Paul Rossignol
	Financial services	Gérard de la Dure
		Paul Rossignol
	Health care	Jackie Tod
	Technology	
	Media, entertainment	Marie-Annick Flambard Guy
	Professional services	Ann-Katrin Dolium
Germany	Automotive, industry	Ulrich Dade
	Consumer	
	Energy, oil	Matthias Ruppert
	Financial services	Joe Defregger
	Health care	Sabine von Anhalt
		Anja Schelte

	Media, entertainment	Peter Paschek
	Professional services	Burkhard Block
		Werner Lembke
	Technology	Siegfried Lamprecht
		Manfred Schanz
Italy	Automotive, industry	Pierluigi Callerio
	Consumer	Pierpaolo Dalzocchio
		Luigi Mancioppi
	Energy, oil	Pierluigi Callerio
		Luigi Mancioppi
	Financial services	Frédérique Meyer
	Health care	Antonio Pellerano
	Media, entertainment	Pierpaolo Dalzocchio
	Professional services	Luigi Mancioppi
	Technology	Pierpaolo Dalzocchio
		Luigi Mancioppi
Netherlands	Automotive, industry	Harry Kunzel
		Andrew Rommes
		Jacques Schoonbrood
	Consumer	Eelco van Eijck
		Andrew Rommes
	Energy, oil	Rochus van der Weg
	Financial services	Tim Kloosterman
	Health care	Eelco van Eijck
	Media, entertainment	Eelco van Eijck
		Andrew Rommes
	Professional services	Jan Lubbers
	Technology	Harry Kunzel
Russia	Automotive, industry	Sophie Vergnas
	Consumer	Ekaterina Kimpelainen
	Financial services	Ekaterina Kimpelainen
		Sophie Vergnas
		Andrea Wine
	Industry	Sophie Vergnas
		Andrea Wine
	Health care	Anton Storozhenko
	Professional services	
	Technology	
Spain	Family business	Luis Conde

	Financial services	Eduardo Conde
		José Loring
	Professional services	Abel Gibert
Sweden	Automotive, industry	Hans-Erik Werthén
	Consumer	Svein Ruud
	Energy, oil	Göran Brittsjö
	Financial services	Magnus Carlsson
	Health care	Ulf Assargard
	Media, entertainment	Svein Ruud
	Professional services	Carin Wiklund Plyhm
	Technology	Johan Nyberg
Switzerland	Health care	Eugenie Centonze
UK	Consumer	Paula Alexander
	Financial & professional services	Trish Miller
	Health care	Sarah Orwin
	Media, entertainment	Stephen Bampfylde
	Technology	Caroline Firstbrook

North America

Canada	Automotive, industry	George Enns
	Consumer	Judi Hutchinson
	Financial services	Bob Dolan
	Health care	Rita Eskudt
	Media, entertainment	
	Professional services	Anne Marie Turnbull
	Technology	Jock McGregor
US		
Atlanta	Automotive, industry	Gary Daugherty
	Consumer	Dan Parker
	Energy, oil	
	Financial services	
	Health care	
	Media, entertainment	
	Professional services	
	Technology	Dan Parker
		Laurie Wilder
Detroit	Automotive, industry	Paul Czamanske
Chicago	Consumer, retail	Jerry Lipe
	Health care	Linda Cook
	Technology	Peter Czamanske

Latin America

Argentina	Automotive, industry Energy, oil Financial services Professional services	Mario Franzini
	Consumer	Martina Uranga
	Media, entertainment Technology	Gonzalo Guerrico
Brazil	Automotive, industry Energy, oil	Luiz Panelli
	Consumer	Luciano Carbonari
	Family business	Luis Cabrera
	Financial services	Antonio Motta
	Health care	Guilherme Velloso
	Media, entertainment	Luis Cabrera Guilherme Velloso
	Professional services	Luciano Carbonari Antonio Motta
	Technology	Paulo Feliciano
Colombia	Consumer	Ricardo Bayona
	Energy, oil Financial services Technology	Roberto E. Hall
	Health care	Carlos E. Hall
	Media, entertainment	Ricardo Bayona
Mexico City	Automotive, industry Technology	Maria Elena Juarez
	Consumer	Pablo Francis Maria Elena Juarez José Luis Newman
	Financial services Media, entertainment	José Luis Newman
	Health care	Pablo Francis
Mexico (Monterrey)	Automotive, industry	José Carrillo Gutierrez Gabriela Jauregui
	Consumer	José Carrillo Gutierrez
	Family business	Cosme Furlong Madero
	Financial services	Ramiro Hernández
	Professional services Technology	Dario Treviño Muguerza

Venezuela	Automotive, industry Energy, oil	Roberto Drew-Bear
	Consumer Health care	Robert Crease
	Technology	Robert Crease Roberto Drew-Bear

Asia & Australasia

Australia	Automotive, industry	Richard King
	Consumer	Rob Pocknee
	Energy, oil	Craig Mahony
	Financial services	Craig Mahony Rob Pocknee
	Health care	Sean Davies
	Media, entertainment	Rob Southey
	Professional services	Sean Davies Craig Mahony Rob Pocknee
	Technology	Ian Cordiner Craig Mahony
China	Automotive, industry Energy, oil Health care	Addy Lee
	Consumer Media, entertainment Professional services Technology	Luo Ming
	Financial services	Louise Ho
India	Automotive, industry	Atul Kumar
	Consumer Health care Media, entertainment	Preety Kumar
	Energy, oil Financial services Professional services	Sanjay Kapoor
	Technology	Atul Kumar
Japan	Automotive, industry Consumer	Takashi Mochizuki
	Energy, oil Professional services Technology	Nobuyuki Tsuji

	Financial services	Yoichi Nakano
	Health care	
New Zealand	Automotive, industry	Elaine McCaw
	Family business	
	Financial services	
	Media, entertainment	
	Professional services	
	Consumer	Lilias Bell
	Energy, oil	
	Health care	
	Technology	
Singapore	Automotive, industry	Aston Goh
	Consumer	
	Financial services	Aston Goh
		Tan Soo Jin
	Energy, oil	Bob Gattie
	Media, entertainment	Bob Gattie
		Wong Jee Tu
	Health care	Bob Gattie
		Aston Goh
	Professional services	Tan Soo Jin
		Wong Jee Tu
	Technology	Aston Goh
		Wong Jee Tu
Taiwan	Automotive, industry	William Hsu
	Consumer	Manny Lopez
	Health care	
	Media, entertainment	
	Professional services	
	Family business	Julianne Wang
	Financial services	
	Technology	William Hsu
Thailand	Automotive, industry	Michael Ascot
	Consumer	
	Family business	
	Financial services	Sivaporn Halidsadeekul
	Technology	

The Globe Search Group

Senior management

Chairman ....Miles Broadbent
Co-ordinator, UK ....Guy Beresford
Co-ordinator, Europe ....Christoph Zeiss
Co-ordinator, US ....Brian Meany

Headquarters

North America
Herbert Mines Associates
375 Park Avenue, Suite 301
New York, NY 10152
US
Tel: +1 212 355 0909

Europe
The Miles Partnership
19–21 Old Bond Street
London W1S 4PX
UK
Tel: +44 20 7495 7772

Europe
Hofmann & Heads! AG & Co
Karlsplatz 5
80335 Munich
Germany
Telephone: +49 89 515 5590

Websites

www.globesearchgroup.com
www.herbertmines.com
www.miles-partnership.com
www.hofman-heads.com

Office locations

(Some cities have more than one office)

Europe	Copenhagen, Frankfurt/Koenigstein, London, Munich, Oslo, Paris, Stockholm, Warsaw
Americas	New York, Palo Alto, San Francisco, Toronto
Asia & Australasia	Melbourne, Sydney

Practice groups

Consumer goods and retail
Financial services
Higher education and not-for-profit
Industrial, manufacturing, chemicals
  and energy

Life sciences and health care
Technology and telecommunications
Support services

Services offered

Executive search   Leadership assessment
Board of directors recruiting

Global performance data

Figures are for 2004
Net revenue $76m
Number of partners   69[a]
Number of researchers   72[b]
Net revenue per consultant $1.1m
Number of offices worldwide   17
% change in net revenue 2003/04   23

a Includes consultants. b Includes associates.

Global net revenue by industry sector (%)
Consumer goods, retail   27
Higher education, non-for-profit   6
Financial services   12
Life sciences, health care   13
Industrial, manufacturing, chemicals, energy   19
Professional & business services   11
Technology, telecommunications   12

Global net revenue by function (%)
Board directors   12
General management   28
Finance   18
Information technology   4
Marketing, sales   21
Operations management   12
Senior administration   5

Net revenue by geographic region (%)
Europe, Middle East & Africa   58
North America   37
Asia & Australasia   5

Comments

The Globe Search Group is a network of 14 partner-owned firms, established in 1997 by The Miles Partnership in London (which itself had been in existence since 1966). The group has offices in Europe, North America and Australia. Its particular strengths are in retail, services (such as leisure, hospitality, support services, logistics and outsourcing), consumer packaged goods, fashion-luxury goods, health care and insurance.

Herbert Mines in New York is considered the pre-eminent firm in consumer, retail and fashion in the United States, and Hofman & Heads in Germany is also well known in the consumer and retail fields. The Miles Partnership in London is well respected in board director, CEO and CFO search. A new partner in France, Jouve & Associés, joined the group in 2005. It is a well-respected firm, especially known in consumer, retail, media, publishing, HR and technology.

Sectors and specialists

E-mail address format varies.

Europe	Sector	Consultant
UK	Business-to-business services CFOs Industrial	Guy Beresford
	Health care Property	Simon Bartholomew
	Insurance, retail	Ian Lazarus
	Board directors	Miles Broadbent
	Consumer, retail, leisure	Chris Stainton
	CFOs Consumer, retail, leisure	Nigel Smith
North America		
US	Consumer, CEOs, function heads	Dave Hardie
	E-commerce, retail, legal Real estate	Gene Manheim
	Luxury retail	Cathy Taylor
	Retail, apparel	Bob Nahas, Jane Vergari
	Retail, consumer	Howard Gross Brian Meany Mary McFarren Saxon Harald Reiter

IIC Partners

Senior management

Chairman	Urs Martin Wüthrich, J. Friisberg Robertson & Partners, Zollikon-Zurich
Vice-chairmen	Americas: Graham Carver, Cambridge Management Planning, Toronto
	Europe: Martine Bournerias, Progress Search, Paris
	Asia Pacific: Lim Chye Lian, Executive Talent International, Singapore

Board of directors

Anthony Ainsworth, Richard Glynn Consultants Executive Recruitment, Bangkok
Martine Bournerias
Lim Chye Lian
Kris de Jaeger, Kris de Jaeger & Associates, Sydney
Ginger Napier, Clarey/Napier International, Houston
Tom Schneider
Rick Slayton, Slayton International, Chicago
Chris Stokes, Key2People, Milan
Piotr Wielgomas, BIGRAM Executive Search, Warsaw
Urs Martin Wüthrich

Headquarters

IIC Partners
255 5th Avenue SW, Suite 830
Calgary
Alberta T2P 3G6
Canada
Tel: +1 403 261 8080

Website

www.iicpartners.com

Office locations

Europe	Amsterdam, Bad Homburg, Belfast, Brussels, Copenhagen, Dublin, Dusseldorf, Hamburg, Helsinki, Lisbon, London, Madrid, Milan, Moscow, Munich, Oslo, Padua, Paris, Riga, Stockholm, Stuttgart, Tallinn, Vienna, Vilnius, Warsaw, Zurich
Americas	Atlanta, Calgary, Chicago, Columbus, Curitiba, Denver, Edmonton, Houston, Mexico City, Montreal, New York, Rio de Janeiro, San Diego, São Paulo, Toronto, Washington DC
Asia & Australasia	Auckland, Bangkok, Beijing, Bombay, Hong Kong, Seoul, Shanghai, Singapore, Sydney, Taipei, Tokyo

Practice groups

Automotive	Industrial and manufacturing
Energy	Health sciences
Financial services	Technology

Services offered

All offices are independent, retainer-based executive search companies and the range of other services provided by each office varies

Global performance data

Figures are for 2003/04 financial year

Net revenue	$75.3m
Number of partners	180
Number of researchers	110
Net revenue per consultant	$418,333
Number of offices worldwide	53
% change in net revenue 2003/04	11.3

Net revenue by geographic region (%)

Europe	59
North America	29
Asia & Australasia	9
Latin America	3

Comments

In 1986 representatives of four companies – Christian Dalum (Copenhagen), Karsten Wick (Hamburg), Knut Isachsen (Oslo) and Gerd Wilhelm (Vienna) – met in Copenhagen and founded Independent Consultants International (ICI). The group grew in Europe and by the early 1990s had expanded into the United States and Canada. At this point the name was changed from ICI to IIC Partners and the group expanded throughout Europe, the Americas and Asia.

Despite the recession of the early 2000s, the group grew and the volume of billings increased. In terms of revenue, IIC Partners is one of the top ten global search firms worldwide and the group's "independent entrepreneurs" are well known in many markets.

IIC Partners is actively expanding its presence through its strongest sectors, which include financial services, energy, industrial and automotive. It is already well known in Canada, the United States (Slayton), the UK (Curzon), France (Progress), the Netherlands (Holtrop Ravesloot) and Norway (ISCO). During 2004 the group gained a number of new members with strength in financial services including Xecutive in Hong Kong, FESA in Brazil, Harris Associates in the United States, Elbinger in Austria, Hoffman in Belgium and Merc in Ireland.

The Curzon Partnership in London and other partners in Calgary, Houston and Moscow are well known in the energy sector. Prominent in the industrial and manufacturing sector are Urs Martin Wüthrich (Zurich), Slayton & Partners (Chicago), Harris (Columbus), IIC Partners (Germany) and Palson (Tokyo). Australian, American and German partners are well represented in the automotive sector.

IIC Partners wants to strengthen its sector/practice groups worldwide and acknowledges that one of the challenges is to identify new and qualified partners in areas where the group is not yet represented.

Sectors and specialists

E-mail address format varies.

Europe	Sector	Consultant
Austria	Life sciences	Peter Eblinger
Belgium	Industrial	Ineke Arts
	Life sciences	Myriam Walgraef
France	Automotive	Thierry Sinquin
	Financial services	Martine Bournerias
		Jean Prieur
	Life sciences	Jean-Marie Faraggi

	Technology	Corinne Handelsman
Germany	Financial services	Juergen Gleue (Hamburg) Christoph von Nostitz (Munich)
	Industry	Rolf C. Stein
	Life sciences	Christoph von Nostitz
	Technology	Helmut R. Haug
Ireland	Life sciences	John Glenny
Italy	Financial services	Francesco Benvenuti
	Industry	Giordano Tamagni
	Life sciences	Luca Temellini
Norway	Energy	Christian Blaauw
Russia	Energy	Viacheslav (Slava) Volkov
Spain	Financial services	Pedro Moreno De Los Rios
Switzerland	Financial services	Rolf Frick
UK	Automotive	Carol Palmer
	Energy	Lachlan Rhodes
	Financial services	David Timson
	Life sciences	Simon Coxon
	Technology	Malcolm Thorp

North America
Canada

Calgary	Energy	Jim Conroy
		Peter Edwards
Montreal	Life sciences	Richard M. Matte

US

Chicago	Automotive	John Nimesheim
	Industry	Rick Slayton
Columbus	Financial services	Jeffrey Harris
Houston	Energy	Bill Clarey
San Diego	Life sciences	Stacey L. Davenport
Washington	Technology	Paul Dinte
		Chris Sunday

Latin America

Brazil	Energy	Michael Lawrence
	Financial services	Alfredo Assumpcao
	Life sciences	Denys Monteiro

Asia & Australasia

Australia	Automotive	Kris de Jager
	Industry	
	Life sciences	John McGee
Hong Kong	Financial services	Marco Foehn
	Industry	Ivo A. Hahn
Japan	Automotive	Koichi Sakamoto
	Life sciences	
Korea	Life sciences	Song-Hyon Jang
New Zealand	Consumer	Bryan Dyke
	Financial services	Mark Porath
Singapore	Financial services	Nicolas Copp
	Life sciences	Lim Chye Lian
	Technology	

Transsearch International

Senior management
Chairman . . . . .Alain Tanugi
North America . . . . .Steven Pezim
Europe, Middle East, Africa . . .Tord Steffenson, Ulrich Ackermann
Asia Pacific . . . . .Vincent Swift
Latin America . . . . .Ewaldo Endler

Board of directors
Ulrich Ackermann   Tord Steffenson
Claudio Crosta   Vincent Swift
Gerhardt Oberlechner   Alain Tanugi
Alain Roca

Headquarters
37–39 rue Boissière
75116 Paris
France
Tel: +33 1 4434 2068

Website: www.transearch.com

Office locations
(Some cities have more than one office)

Europe	Amsterdam, Barcelona, Brussels, Budapest, Copenhagen, Dornbirn, Dublin, Frankfurt, Geneva, Gothenburg, Helsinki, Innsbruck, Lille, Limerick, Lisbon, London, Madrid, Milan, Munich, Oslo, Paris, Stockholm, Stuttgart, Warsaw, Zurich
Americas	Caracas, Charlotte, Chicago, Dallas, Denver, Houston, Kansas City, Lima, Mexico City, Montreal, New York, Santiago, São Paulo, Toronto
Asia & Australasia	Bangkok, Hong Kong, Kuala Lumpur, New Delhi, Seoul, Shanghai, Sydney, Tokyo
Middle East & Africa	Johannesburg, Kuwait City

Practice groups

Automotive, industrial and supply chain	Not-for-profit
	Life sciences
Boards and non-executive directors	Media and publishing
Consumer, retail and fashion	Professional services and consulting
Energy and resources	Technology
Financial services	

Services offered

Executive search	Management audit

Global performance data

Figures are for 2003 unless stated otherwise

Net revenue	$70m[a]
Number of partners	145[b]
Number of researchers	82
Net revenue per consultant	$344,985
Number of offices worldwide	53
% change in net revenue 2003/04	n/a

a 2004 estimate. b Number of consultants.

Net revenue by geographic region (%)	
Europe, Africa, Middle East	58
North America	23
Asia Pacific	15
Latin America	3

Comments

Transearch International was established in 1982 in London with founders based in the UK, France and Germany. Alain Tanugi, one of the founders, has been chairman for 18 years. Today it is a global consortium of locally owned firms with 53 offices in 35 countries. In terms of size, the firm is ranked in the top ten and has worked at tightening its network and improving quality control procedures.

Tanugi revitalised the group's UK office with the affiliation of Norman Broadbent, and Cromwell Partners (a financial services specialist in New York) joined the group in 2004. It is also planning to build its presence in other American markets. The group's profile is growing in Asia, where two new offices opened in 2004 in New Delhi and Shanghai. There are also plans to open offices in Beijing and in Bratislava,

Moscow and Prague, as the group addresses the need to strengthen its presence in eastern Europe.

Transearch operates a matrix structure, in which it is organised by geography, industry specialisation and functional expertise as well as by leadership services. Industry specialisation is well covered with a focus on all the main areas. It has an excellent reputation in technology and life sciences. Future plans include the strengthening of the financial services group with the inclusion of legal and insurance specialisations.

The strategy for growth is based on promoting better brand awareness and on franchising new offices around the world in a consistent way, while providing strong central support for local offices with a permanently employed staff providing business development, marketing and technology services.

Sectors and consultants

All e-mail addresses follow the same format: firstname.lastname@ transearch.com (eg, gerhardt.oberlechner@transearch.com)

Europe	Sector	Consultant
Austria	Consumer	Gerhardt Oberlechner
	Health care	Astrid Fleischhacker
Belgium	Financial services	Philippe van Heurck
	Health care	Karine Becker
	Technology	
Denmark	Health care	Christian Enghave
	Technology	
Finland	Technology	Mikael Charpentier
France	Automotive, industry	Jean Bousser
		Christian de Charrette
		Edouard-Nicolas Dubar
	Consumer	Daniel Arnoux
		Jean Bousser
		Dominique Willem
	Fashion, luxury goods	Gilbert Personeni
	Energy, oil	Christian de Charrette
	Financial services	Arnaud de Courson
	Health care	Véronique Dugué
	Legal	Gatien Job
	Media, entertainment	Alain Roca
	Technology	Alain Roca
		François Le Grin

Germany	Automotive, industry	Gerhard Swierzy
		Roland Rabe
	Consumer	Ulrich Ackermann
		Roland Rabe
	Financial services	Johanna Häfner
	Health care	Gerhard Swierzy
		Johanna Häfner
	Industry	Hans Berg
	Media, entertainment	Roland Rabe
	Technology	Ulrich Ackermann
Hungary	Technology	Laszlo Toth
Ireland	Health care	John Harty
		Conor Harty
	Technology	Jerry O'Keefe
		Liam McDonnell
Italy	Automotive, industry	Giuseppe Biffis
	Consumer	Claudio Crosta
	Health care	Claudio Fertonani
		Marco Fertonani
		Rino Nucci
	Technology	Mario Jesi
Netherlands	Automotive, industry	Ernst Advocaat
	Health care	Michel de Boer
	Technology	Ernst Advocaat
Norway	Automotive, industry	John Endsjoe
	Energy, oil	
Poland	Consumer	François Nail
	Technology	
Portugal	Automotive, industry	Soledade Morais
	Health care	
South Africa	Energy, oil	Ian Blackie
Spain	Automotive, industry	Julio Amo
	Health care	
Sweden	Automotive, industry	C.G. Carlebom
	Consumer	Jan Jaldeland
	Financial services	Per Synnes
	Health care	Tord Steffenson
	Industry	Roland Johnsson
	Technology	Bertil Helzel
		Lisbeth Holm

Switzerland	Financial services	Heinrich Stampfli
		Hazeline von Swaay
	Health care	Hazeline von Swaay
	Technology	Lea Sauer
UK	Energy, oil	Andrew Lees
	Financial services	Lynne Hall
		Alex Davies
	Industry, supply chain	Beth Cauldwell
		Bill Greenwell
	Health care	Edward Docherty
	Legal	Nicholas Woolf
	Media, entertainment	Ian Johnston
	Professional services	Nicholas Woolf
	Technology	Jon Letts
		Phil Peters

North America

Canada	Consumer	Joel Fatum
	Energy, oil	Russ Buckland
	Health care	Howard Pezim
	Media, entertainment	Michel Pauzé
		Steven Pezim
	Technology	Steven Pezim
US	Automotive, industry	Audrey Hellinger
	Consumer	Rob Andrews
		Pat Carlucci
		Steve Silva
	Energy, oil	Bob Rollins
	Financial services	Paul Heller
		Audrey Hellinger
		Dylan Magee
		Bob Sherrill
		Joe Ziccardi
	Health care	Rich Parker
		Peter Lemke
		Audrey Hellinger
	Technology	Gary Green

Latin America

Brazil	Automotive, industry	Grace Pedreira
	Consumer	Ewaldo Endler
	Technology	
Chile	Consumer	Cristian Duarte
		Oscar Anwandter
Mexico	Technology	Agustin Flores
Peru	Automotive, industry	Jorge Velaochaga
	Energy, oil	
Venezuela	Consumer	Rosa Maria Herrera
	Energy, oil	

Asia & Australasia

Australia	Consumer	Randall Maple
		Russell Reeves
	Energy, oil	Bob Lewy
	Technology	Randall Maple
China	Automotive, industry	Vincent Swift
	Consumer	
	Health care	James Koh
	Industry	
	Technology	James Koh
		Vincent Swift
Korea	Automotive, industry	Yeon Joo Koo
		James Kim
	Consumer	Yeon Joo Koo
	Financial services	K. Park
	Technology	Julia Park
Malaysia	Automotive, industry	Wendy Lau
	Technology	
Thailand	Consumer	Taeil Chung
	Financial services	Taeil Chung
		John Da Silva
	Oil, gas	Matthew Parson
	Technology	Gary Williams
Japan	Automotive, industry	Haruo Hamaguchi
		Takeharu Kubota
		Tetsuya Kinoshita
	Consumer	Kazuyuki Sasaki
	Health care	

	Financial services	Kenji Tomono
		Tsutomu Kashihara
	Technology	Tetsuya Kinoshita
India	Automotive, industry	Uday Chawla
	Consumer	Atul Vohra
		Sangeeta Pal
		Tejinder Ral Singh
	Financial services	Atul Vohra
	Health care	Guljit Chaudhri
		Uday Chawla
		Tejinder Ral Singh
	Technology	Uday Chawla

Middle East & Africa

| Kuwait | Energy, oil | Hasan Hadeed |
| | Financial services | |

Whitehead Mann Group

Senior management

Managing director . . . . .Chris Merry
Company secretary . . . . .Mark Ground

Board of directors

Jonathan Baines
Sir Hugh Collum
Carol Leonard

Chris Merry
Alan Smith
Sir Colin Southgate (chairman)

Headquarters

Global and Europe
14 Hay's Mews
London W1J 5PT
UK
Tel: +44 20 7290 2000

North America
280 Park Avenue
East Tower, 25th Floor
New York, NY 10017
US
Tel: +1 212 894 8300

Website

www.wmann.com

Office locations

(Excluding affiliates)
Europe   Birmingham, Cirencester, Edinburgh, Frankfurt,
                London, Leeds, Paris
Americas   New York, Colorado Springs
Asia & Australasia   Hong Kong

Practice groups

Boards and non-executives
Consumer and retail
Financial services
Industry
Life sciences

Professional services
Public sector
Technology, media
  and telecommunications

Services offered

Board evaluation
Executive search
Executive coaching
  and development

Executive assessment
Interim management

Global performance data

Figures are for 2003/04 financial year

Net revenue	$61.2m
Number of partners	70
Number of researchers	n/a
Net revenue per consultant	n/a
Number of offices worldwide	12
% change in net revenue 2003/04	−2

Global net revenue by industry sector (%)

Consumer, retail	17
Financial services	45
Health care	4
Industry	12
Professional services	6
Public sector	8
Technology, media and telecoms	8

Global net revenue by function (%)

Assessment	7
Coaching and development	14
Recruitment	80

Net revenue by geographic region (%)

UK	85
Rest of world	11
North America	4

Comments

Whitehead Mann was founded in London in 1971 by Anna and Clive Mann. It was floated on the London stockmarket in 1997 and subsequently acquired a number of firms:

- GKR Group (2000), extending Whitehead Mann's international and sectoral reach;
- The Change Partnership (2001), one of the UK's leading coaching organisations;
- Baines Gwinner (2001), a British financial services specialist, significantly strengthening the group's presence in this sector;
- Summit Leadership Solutions Company (2002), strengthening the group's American coaching and development capability;

☑ Leonard Hull (2004), a board-level search specialist.

The company had a turbulent 2004 with the departure of Anna Mann, approaches (but no offers) from potential buyers followed by profit warnings in late 2004 and early 2005. Its industrial practice group led by Paul Turner is highly rated in the UK and it is also well respected for its public-sector group.

The firm has a broad portfolio of related businesses (search, management assessment and coaching). The Change Partnership, its coaching group, is ranked number one worldwide. In early 2004, the firm started an interim management business.

Whitehead Mann has a number of well-respected affiliates, including GKR Daulet-Singh in India, McDonald Monahan in Australia, Woodburn Mann in South Africa and Simon Monk in New Zealand.

The main challenges facing the group are to reinforce growth in Europe and Asia and to find a way to compete effectively in the United States, where it has only two offices.

Sectors and specialists

All e-mail addresses follow the same format: firstname.lastname@wmann.com (eg, catherine.fleuriot@wmann.com)

Europe	Sector	Consultant
Belgium	Consumer	Catherine Fleuriot
	Energy, oil	Trevor Childs
	Financial services	Valerie Barthes de Ruyter
France	Automotive, industry	Gerard Clery-Melin
	Energy, oil	Jean-Pierre Gouirand
	Consumer	Catherine Fleuriot
	Financial services	Valerie Barthes de Ruyter
	Health care	Sonia D'Emilio (also covers Belgium)
	Media, entertainment	Sonia D'Emilio
	Professional services	Sylvain Dhenin (excluding legal)
	Technology	Sylvain Dhenin (also covers Belgium, Denmark, Italy, Netherlands, Spain, Sweden, Switzerland)

Germany	Consumer Financial services Health care Technology	Peter Behncke
	Professional services	Natascha Antonio (legal) Peter Behncke (other)
Italy	Professional services	Ali Rea (legal)
UK	Automotive, industry	Paul Turner, Toby Lapage-Norris (also cover Belgium, Denmark, Germany, Italy, Netherlands, Spain, Sweden, Switzerland, Canada, US, Australia, Japan)
	Consumer	Samantha Allen (also covers Denmark, Italy, Netherlands, Spain, Sweden, Switzerland, Australia)
	Energy, oil	Paul Turner, Toby Lapage-Norris (also cover Denmark, Germany, Italy, Netherlands, Spain, Sweden, Switzerland, Canada, US, Australia, Japan)
	Financial services	Andrew Simpson (also covers Denmark, Italy, Netherlands, Spain, Sweden, Switzerland, Australia)
	Health care	Chris Burrows (also covers Denmark, Italy, Netherlands, Spain, Sweden, Switzerland, Canada, Australia, China, Japan, India)
	Media, entertainment	Gill Carrick (also covers Belgium, Denmark, Germany, Italy, Netherlands, Spain, Sweden, Switzerland, Canada, Australia, Japan, India)

	Professional services (legal and other)	Anthony May (also covers Belgium, Denmark, France (legal), Italy (other), Netherlands, Spain, Sweden, Switzerland, Canada, US (legal), Australia, India)
	Technology	Graham Jones

North America

US	Consumer	Jim DiFilippo (also covers Canada)
	Financial services	Amy Russo (also covers Canada)
	Health care	Eleanor Thorp
	Media, entertainment	Kay Cioffi
	Professional services	Amy Russo (excluding legal)
	Technology	Kay Cioffi (also covers Canada)

Asia & Australasia

China	Automotive, industry Energy, oil Consumer Financial services	David Hui
	Professional services	David Hui (also covers Japan)
	Media, entertainment	Rachel Tsai
	Technology	David Hui (also covers Australia, Japan, India)
India	Automotive, industry Consumer Energy, oil Financial services	Surendra (Miki) Daulet-Singh

Highland Partners

Senior management (Highland Partners)

```
Chairman  . . . . . . . . . . . . . . . . . . . . . . . . . . . .Michael T. Kelly
President and CEO North America and Europe . .John Wallace
CEO Asia . . . . . . . . . . . . . . . . . . . . . . . . . . . .Dan Dumitrescu
```

Board of directors (Hudson Highland Group)

Jon Chait	Nicholas G. Moore
Richard Pehlke	David G. Offensend
John J. Haley	René Schuster
Jennifer Laing	

Headquarters

North America	*Europe*
622 Third Avenue, 38th Floor	Kinnaird House
New York, NY 10017	1 Pall Mall East
US	London SW1Y 5AU
Tel: +1 212 351 7300	UK
	Tel: +44 20 7451 9400

Websites

www.highlandsearch.com   www.hhgroup.com

Office locations

Europe	London
Americas	Atlanta, Boston, Buenos Aires, Chicago, Dallas, Encino, Los Angeles, Minneapolis, New York, Phoenix, San Francisco, Stamford, Toronto
Asia & Australasia	Hong Kong, Melbourne, Sydney

Practice groups

Industry

Consumer and retail	Life sciences and health care
Financial services	Technology and IT services
Industrial	

Functional

Boards of directors	Human resources
Chief financial officer	Legal
Chief information officer	

157

Services offered

Executive coaching	Internet recruitment
Executive search	Management audit

Global performance data

Figures are for 2003

Net revenue	$60.07m
Number of partners	66
Number of researchers	51
Net revenue per consultant	$910,200
Number of offices worldwide	17[a]
% change in net revenue 2003/04	n/a

a Highland Partners only.

Global net revenue by industry sector (%)

Consumer, retail	16
Financial services	32
Life sciences, health care	19
Industrial	15
Professional services, other	9
Technology & IT services	9

Comments

Highland Partners is the search arm of Hudson Highland, which was formed in 2003. But it has a long history that started in the early 1950s with the founding of Ward Howell and Lamalie, two executive search firms. Lamalie became a public company in 1997 and acquired Ward Howell in 1998. The merged group was renamed LAI-Ward Howell. Then another large firm, TMP, consolidated several search and recruitment firms under its TMP banner, including LAI-Ward Howell, Highland Partners, TASA, Johnson Smith Kniseley and Illsley Bourbonnais. At this point the group had five lines of business:

- internet recruitment (Monster.com);
- advertising (Yellow pages);
- an interactive division;
- global staffing (Hudson);
- search (including Highland Partners).

In April 2003, TMP changed its name from TMP to Monster and split off two of the above groups, global staffing and search. These groups were formed into one company, Hudson Highland, which continued to focus on staffing, HR consulting and search. Hudson Highland is well respected in the fields of financial services and boards (Robert Rollo in Los Angeles) and insurance (Mike and Pat Corey in Chicago). It is also well known for health care under Neal Maslan in Encino, CA, which specialises in health-care service distribution, health-care IT and pharmaceuticals. It has a growing business in retail (based in Atlanta) and is improving its presence in the technology sector in the United States and Asia.

After a series of restructurings, Highland Partners is trying to build a global presence. It is a group of well-known boutique firms in the United States and Canada with a strong presence in financial services and health care, but it has a significant amount of work to do to build its presence in Europe and Asia.

Sectors and specialists

All e-mail addresses follow the same format:
firstname.lastname@hhgroup.com (eg, ulrika.hagle@hhgroup.com)

Europe	Sector	Consultant
Belgium	Health care	Ulrika Hagle
France	Health care	Fallya Petrakopoulou
Switzerland	Automotive, industry	Rainer Faistauer
	Energy, oil	
	Technology	
	Financial services	
	Professional services	Peter Sondereger
UK	Consumer, retail	Martin Kendall
	Health care	Ulrika Hagle
	Media, entertainment	Grace Borrelli
	Professional services	Simon Rhodes
	Technology	Fiona Vickers

North America		
Canada	Automotive, industry	Marcelo Mackinlay
	Consumer, retail	Tanya Van Biesen
	Financial services	
	Energy, oil	Marcelo Mackinlay
	Health care	Bill Probert
	Professional services	Derek Roberts

	Technology	Bernadette Testani
US	Automotive, industry Consumer, retail Energy, oil	Bud Wright
	Financial services	Mike Corey
	Health care	Mike Kelly
	Media, entertainment	Judy Stubbs
	Professional services Technology	Jim Bethmann
	Human resources	Darren Romano
	Board of directors	Robert Rollo
	Legal	Kristin Hebert

Asia & Australasia

Australia	Automotive, industry	Mark Lelliott
	Consumer, retail	Deborah Willsher
	Energy, oil Technology	Mark Lelliott
	Financial services	Catherine Anderson
	Health care Media, entertainment	Julie Perigo
	Professional services	Jason Johnson

A.T. Kearney Executive Search

Senior management

President ....G. Stephen Fisher (primary contact for
                                    Americas)
Chairman ....Paul Menmuir (primary contact for Europe)
Vice-chairman ....Paul Ray Jr (primary contact for Asia Pacific)

Headquarters

North America
A.T. Kearney Inc
Executive Search Division
222 W. Adams Street
Chicago, IL 60606
US
Telephone: +1 312 648 0111

Europe
A.T. Kearney Limited
Executive Search Division
Lansdowne House
Berkeley Square
London W1J 6ER
UK
Tel: +44 20 7468 8000

Website

www.executivesearch.atkearney.com

Office locations

Europe	Amsterdam, Brussels, Dusseldorf, Frankfurt, Geneva, London, Madrid, Milan, Munich, Oslo, Paris, Stockholm
Americas	Alexandria, Atlanta, Chicago, Costa Mesa, Fort Worth, Los Angeles, Miami ,New York, Plano, São Paulo, Silicon Valley, Stamford, Toronto
Asia & Australasia	Hong Kong, Singapore, Sydney, Tokyo

Practice groups

Consumer goods and retail
Financial services
Higher education and not-for-profit
Industrial, manufacturing, chemicals
  and energy

Life sciences and health care
Technology and telecommunications

Services offered

Board of directors recruiting
Consulting services via A.T. Kearney
  Management Consultants

Executive search
Leadership assessment
Succession planning

Global performance data

Figures are for 2003 unless stated otherwise

Net revenue	$44.8m[a]
Number of partners	84[b]
Number of researchers	76
Net revenue per consultant	$465,476
Number of offices worldwide	29
% change in net revenue 2003/04	14.6

a 2004. b Includes consultants.

Global net revenue by industry sector (%)

Consumer goods and retail	13
Higher education and not-for-profit	15
Financial services	16
Industrial, manufacturing, chemicals and energy	19
Life sciences and health care	14
Professional and business services	4
Technology and telecommunications	19

Global net revenue by function (%)

Financial services	16
General management	28
Information technology	10
Marketing and sales	23
Operations management	12
Senior administration	11

Net revenue by geographic region (%)

Americas	67
Europe, Africa and Middle East	28
Asia and Australasia	5

Comments

A.T. Kearney Executive Search was founded in 1946 in Chicago. The firm is a business unit of A.T. Kearney Inc, one of the oldest management consulting firms. A.T. Kearney Inc was purchased by EDS, a global computer services firm, in 1995. At the time EDS was a wholly owned subsidiary of General Motors, but it is now an independent company listed on the New York Stock Exchange.

The linkage of a search firm to a global management consulting firm is unique among search firms, and A.T. Kearney believes that this gives it a different perspective on the strategy and industry dynamics in a wide range of industries and functions. However, some people are concerned that there might be conflicts of interest between search and consulting.

At present, A.T. Kearney Executive Search is among the 15 largest global players, with 29 offices in 17 countries, of which 13 are in the Americas, 12 in Europe and 4 in Asia. It grew from its American base, opening offices in Europe during the 1980s and in Asia during the 1990s. A continuing challenge for the firm, however, is to build its global brand and increase its scale in the markets where it maintains offices. During 2002–03, the company increased its presence in Europe.

All offices are wholly owned and the firm operates as one global profit centre, thus eliminating some of the potential conflicts resulting from cross-border assignments when there are multiple profit centres. A.T. Kearney commits significant resources to the training and development of its consultants and is especially well known for its work in the professional services, technology, operations and supply chain sectors.

Sectors and specialists

All e-mail addresses follow the same format: firstname.lastname@
es.atkearney.com (eg, annie.bingham@es.atkearney.com)

Europe	Sector	Consultant
Belgium	Automotive, industry	Marie-Paule Kirscht
	Health care	
	Technology	
France	Automotive, industry	Jean-Michel Paulhac
	Consumer	Fariman Felisa
	Fashion, retail, luxury goods	Annie Bingham
	Financial services	Jean-François Monteil
	Health care	Priscilla Motte
Germany	Automotive, industry	Martin Schubert (Dusseldorf)
	Financial services	Christian Groh (Frankfurt)
		Willem-Christian Helkenberg (Munich)
	Professional services	Martin Schubert (Dusseldorf)
	Technology	Ansgar Dierkes (Frankfurt)
Italy	Automotive, industry	Alessandro Tosi
	Financial services	

	Health care	Riccardo Kustermann
	Leadership assessment	
	Technology	
	Professional services	Alessandro Tosi
	Technology	Riccardo Kustermann
Norway	Automotive, industry	Thorvald Reinertsen
	Board practice	
	Energy, oil	
	Leadership assessment	
	Consumer	
	Financial services	Tor Lian
	Health care	
Netherlands	Consumer	Jan Schaap
	Energy, oil	
	Financial services	
	Technology	
Spain	Consumer	Joaquin Barallat
	Energy, oil	
	Professional services	
	Leadership assessment	Gustavo Franchella
	Technology	
Sweden	Automotive, industry	Hakan Svennerstal
	Financial services	
	Leadership assessment	
Switzerland	Consumer	Claire Besançon
	Financial services	
	Health care	
UK	Automotive, industry	Geoffrey Walker
	Board practice	Hilary Sears
	Consumer	
	Leadership assessment	
	Energy, oil	Geoffrey Walker
	Financial services	Jonathan Dancy
		James D'Arcy
		Tony Marshall
	Health care	Chris Seabourne
		John Weeks
	Media, entertainment	Hilary Sears
	Professional services	Beth Knight
	Technology	
	Public, not-for-profit	Robin Murray Brown

North America

Canada	Automotive, industry	Jack Harris
		Virginia Murray
	Consumer	Virginia Murray
	Financial services	Mark Ross
	Health care	Jack Harris
	Leadership assessment	Jack Harris
		Virginia Murray
	Professional services	Mark Ross
	Technology	Eva Kaufmann
US		
Alexandria	Education	Charles Bunting
		Shelley Storbeck
Atlanta	Automotive, industry	Richard Citarella
		Ernest Taylor
	Health care	Stephen Dezember
		Deborah Seltzer
	Professional services	Stephen Dezember
Chicago	Automotive, industry	Brad Berke
		Ben DeBerry
		Michelle Smead
		Frank Smeekes
		Frank Steck
	Board practice	Ben DeBerry
	Consumer	Ben DeBerry
		Steve Fisher
		Mary Lou Gorno
		Bob Tate
	Financial services	Alvin Spector
	Health care	Terry Scherck III
		Jim Whittle
Cleveland	Health care	Tim O'Donnell
Costa Mesa	Professional services	Matt Pierce
	Technology	
Fort Worth	Board practice	Paul Ray Jr
	Consumer	
	Technology	Renee Arrington
Los Angeles	Education	Alberto Pimentel
Miami	Automotive, industry	David Lauderback

	Consumer	John Mestepey
	Financial services	
New York	Consumer	Ellery Gordon
		Ric Comins
	Financial services	Russ Gerson
		Robert Holt
		Steve McPherson
		Ken Rich
	Technology	Robert Holt
		Lisa Hooker
Plano	Consumer	David Love
	Financial services	David Hart
		Steve Jordan
	Professional services	Scott Williams
	Technology	Sky Page
Redwood Shores	Technology	John Holland
		Maggie Yen George
Stamford	Automotive, industry	Mark McMahon
	Board practice	Marcia Pryde
		Lisa Tromba
	Financial services	F. Clawson Smith

Asia & Australasia

Australia	Consumer	Karen Fifer
	Professional services	
	Financial services	Sean Linkson
	Education	Karen Fifer
		Sean Linkson
China, Hong Kong,	Automotive, industry	David Chan (Hong Kong)
Singapore	Technology	Steve Hendryx (Fort Worth)
	Consumer	Carolyn Chan (Singapore)
		Steve Hendryx (Fort Worth)
	Financial services	John Carroll (Singapore)
	Health care	Steve Hendryx (Fort Worth)
	Professional services	Carolyn Chan (Singapore)
Japan	Consumer	Masako Kimura
	Health care	Walt Ames
	Media, entertainment	
	Professional services	
	Technology	Masako Kimura

Signium International

Senior management

CEO and chairman of the board . . . . .Bernd Prasuhn
Presidents and regional speakers . . .Americas: Juraci de Andrade
Europe and Africa: Martin McEvoy
Asia Pacific: Jesus M. Zulueta Jr

Board of directors

Bernd Prasuhn
Martin McEvoy
Göran Willner
Glenn G. Anderson Jr

Juraci de Andrade
Piotr Pilecki
Jesus M. Zulueta Jr
Suzanne Speight

Headquarters

360 Memorial Drive, Suite 120
Crystal Lake
IL 60014
US
Tel: +1 815 479 9415

Website

www.signium.com

Office locations

Europe	Amsterdam, Copenhagen, Dublin, Dusseldorf, Helsinki, Gothenburg, Milan, Malmo, Munich, Stockholm, Turku, Vienna, Wroclaw, Zurich
Americas	Chicago, Cleveland, Miami, São Paulo, Tampa
Asia & Australasia	Auckland, Kuala Lumpur, Manila, Seoul, Tokyo, Wellington

Services offered

Executive search
Executive coaching (some offices)
Management assessment
HR consulting

Global performance data

Figures are for 2003

Net revenue	$43.1m
Number of partners	62
Number of researchers	23
Net revenue per consultant	$695,000
Number of offices worldwide	25
% change in net revenue 2003/04	n/a

Global net revenue by industry sector (%)

Automotive, industrial	32
Boards, non-executives	5
Consumer, retail	10
Energy, oil	2
Financial services	5
Foundations, not-for-profit	1
Pharmaceuticals, health care, biotechnology	8
Professional services, consulting	20
Technology	17

Net revenue by geographic region (%)

Europe, Africa & Middle East	78
Asia & Australasia	17
North America	3
Latin America	2

Comments

Ward Howell International Group was founded in the early 1970s by Wardwell Howell, a McKinsey consultant and one of the pioneers of the executive search profession. One of the first international alliances to be formed, it was similar in structure to global law firms where local companies join an existing network.

In 1998, during a period of multiple mergers, acquisitions and public offerings in the executive search industry, Ward Howell in the United States was acquired by LAI, a publicly owned competitor, which was in turn acquired by TMP, a publicly held industry outsider. The American acquisition resulted in the loss of the international group's brand and company name. At this time of sweeping change, the remaining group members (all the global offices apart from the American firm) took the opportunity to rebrand themselves as Signium International.

The group is continuing to build on this brand and increase its international network.

Signium currently ranks in the top 15 firms in the world by revenue. The group has a growing presence in Europe and Asia and is currently targeting its expansion efforts on markets such as France, Spain, the UK, Canada, Mexico, the United States, Australia and China in order to serve regional and global clients. It is also building awareness of the Signium brand through increased activity within the industry (professional associations and conferences) and to clients through targeted marketing.

Sectors and consultants

E-mail address format varies.

Europe	Sector	Consultant
Austria	Automotive, industry Technology	Herbert Ecker
	Consumer	Natalie Ecker
	Professional services	Herbert Ecker Natalie Ecker
Denmark	Consumer Technology	Jan Bach Schjolin
	Health care	Claes Nielsen
Finland	Automotive, industry Consumer	Tor Nygren
	Health care Technology	Tomas Holm
Germany	Automotive, industry	Horst Neller Rolf Dahlems Heinz Juchmes Jutta Lohkampff
	Consumer	Bernd Prasuhn Frances Kelly
	Financial services	Hans Jürgen Etterich Frances Kelly
	Health care	Hans Jürgen Etterich
	Professional services	Jutta Lohkampff
	Technology	Heinz Juchmes Bernd Prasuhn
Ireland	Automotive, industry	Sarah Meagher

	Financial services	
	Technology	
	Consumer	
	Professional services	Martin McEvoy
Italy	Automotive, industry	Lucio de Luca
	Financial services	Gianni dell'Orto
	Health care	
	Professional services	Lucio de Luca
Netherlands	Automotive, industry	Bert van der Wijk
	Financial services	
	Professional services	
	Media, entertainment	Daniel Bos
Poland	Automotive, industry	Piotr Pilecki
	Consumer	
	Financial services	Jowita Oczkowicz
	Health care	Tomasz Szaynok
	Technology	
Sweden	Automotive, industry	Tommy Jansson
		Börje Magnusson
		Göran Willner
	Consumer	Börje Magnusson
	Health care	Linda Gadd
	Professional services	Eva Edlund
	Technology	Eva Edlund
		Göran Willner
Switzerland	Consumer	Nicolas Engels
		Karl-Heinz Harzheim
	Media, entertainment	Karl-Heinz Harzheim
North America		
US	Automotive, industry	Glenn G. Anderson Jr
	Consumer	Walter Baker
	Professional services	Walter Baker
Latin America		
Brazil	Automotive, industry	Juraci de Andrade
	Consumer	Paulo Valin
	Financial services	Gilson E.G. Coehlo
		Juraci de Andrade
	Health care	Paulo Valin

	Technology	Gilson E.G. Coehlo
		Paulo Valin

Asia & Australasia		
Japan	Automotive, industry	Yoichi Asaoka
		Kenji Sakamoto
	Consumer	Toru Fukui
		Kenji Sakamoto
	Health care	Toru Fukui
Korea	Automotive, industry	Peter Manlik
	Health care	
	Financial services	Kang-Shik Koh
	Technology	
Malaysia	Automotive, industry	May T. Lim
	Financial services	
	Technology	
New Zealand	Automotive, industry	Stephen Ellett
	Consumer	Maurice C. Ellett
	Professional services	
Philippines	Automotive, industry	Jose Balderama
	Energy, oil	
	Consumer	Jose Balderama
		Jesus M. Zulueta Jr
	Financial services	Chicho Chuaquico
	Professional services	Jesus M. Zulueta Jr
	Technology	Chicho Chuaquico

Stanton Chase International

Senior management

Chairman . . . . .Steve B. Watson
International treasurer . . . . . .George Cross
Vice-presidents . . . . .North America: Mickey Matthews
Europe, Middle East and Africa: Gert Herold
Latin America: Claudio Fernaud
Asia Pacific: R. Suresh

Headquarters

North America
Stanton Chase Dallas
Two Lincoln Centre
5420 LBJ Freeway, Suite 780
Dallas, TX 75240
US
Tel: +1 972 404 8411

Europe
Stanton Chase International Vienna
Kärntner Ring 5-7
1190 Vienna
Austria
Tel: +43 1 516 260

Website

www.stantonchase.com

Office locations

Europe — Amsterdam, Athens, Belgrade, Bucharest, Budapest, Copenhagen, Frankfurt, Ljubljana, London, Lyon, Madrid, Milan, Paris, Prague, Vienna, Warsaw, Zurich

Americas — Atlanta, Austin, Baltimore, Buenos Aires, Bogota, Caracas, Chicago, Dallas, Denver, Lima, Los Angeles, Mexico City, Miami, Montevideo, New York, Rio de Janeiro, San Francisco, Santa Barbara, Santiago, São Paulo, Toronto

Asia & Australasia — Bangkok, Beijing, Brisbane, Chengdu, Chennai, Guangzhou, Hong Kong, Jakarta, Kuala Lumpur, Manila, Mumbai, Pune, Seoul, Shanghai, Singapore, Sydney, Taipei, Tokyo

Practice groups

Board and governance
Consumer products and services
Financial services
Health care and pharmaceuticals

Manufacturing and engineering
Natural resources and energy
Professional services
Technology

Services offered

Executive search	Management audit
Board director search	

Global performance data

Figures are for 2004	
Net revenue	$39m
Number of partners	156[a]
Number of researchers	150[b]
Net revenue per consultant	$250,000
Number of offices worldwide	56
% change in net revenue 2003/04	n/a

a Includes consultants. b Number of support staff.

Global net revenue by industry sector (%)

Advanced technology	17
Consumer products and services	13
Financial services	19
Health care and pharmaceuticals	9
Manufacturing and engineering	23
Natural resources and energy	5
Professional services	8
Other	7

Net revenue by geographic region (%)

Asia & Australasia	35
Europe	31
North America	24
Latin America	10

Comments

Stanton Chase International was established in Europe and the United States in 1990, although many of the member firms were operating before then. It has since grown and now has 56 offices in 36 countries and is positioned as one of the top 20 executive search firms worldwide as measured by net revenue. The firm is owned by the local offices.

Stanton Chase has a particularly strong presence in developing markets. In 2003, it gained 16 offices in Asia when Bó Lè Associates, a prominent regional search firm, joined the network. This affiliation makes the firm the largest in the region and one of the leading recruiters in China.

In the same year, Ward Howell Euroselect joined Stanton Chase. As a search pioneer in central and eastern Europe, Ward Howell bought over ten years of experience in the region and offices in Budapest, Bucharest, Ljubljana, Prague, Vienna, Warsaw and Zurich. Response, an independent Greek firm based in Athens, also joined the network in 2003. Stanton Chase has established a strong position in Latin American markets with offices in eight countries in the region.

The firm sees its best growth opportunities coming from China, India and eastern Europe where it already has a foothold.

Sectors and specialists

E-mail address format varies.

Europe	Sector	Consultant
Austria	FMCG, retail	Gert Herold
	Manufacturing, engineering	
	Manufacturing, engineering	Alexander Kail
	Financial services	Gerald Mayer
	Manufacturing, engineering	Werner Zeugswetter
	Technology	
Czech Republic	FMCG, retail	Marek Huml
	Professional services	Jozef Papp
	Technology	Thomas Kubalek
Denmark	Manufacturing, engineering	Erik Mikkelsen
France		
Lyon	FMCG, retail	Carole De Chilly
	Financial services	Francis Rouhier
	Technology	
Paris	Manufacturing, engineering	Jean-Claude Attenti
	Professional services	
Germany	Financial services	Erik Meyer
	Health care, pharmaceuticals	
	FMCG, retail	Knut Hofmann
	Manufacturing, engineering	Rudolf Leiwesmeier
	Professional services	Gerd Schmidt
	Technology	Johann Joachim Barring
Greece	Financial services	Manos Panorios
	Health care, pharmaceuticals	Harry Pezoulas
	FMCG, retail	Georgia Kartsanis
	Manufacturing, engineering	
	Technology	Athena Tavoulari

Italy	Financial services	Paolo Pellini
	Health care, pharmaceuticals	
	Manufacturing, engineering	Gian Balbi
Netherlands	FMCG, retail	Frank Boting
	Health care, pharmaceuticals	
	Financial services	Peter Crul
	Professional services	
	FMCG, retail	Peter De Jong
	Health care, pharmaceuticals	
	Manufacturing, engineering	Ludo Houben
	Resources, energy	
	Manufacturing, engineering	Floris Jansen
	Professional services	
Poland	Health care, pharmaceuticals	Anita Malanowicz
	Financial services	Beata Sokolowska-Pek
	FMCG, retail	
Spain	Hospitality, travel	Rafael Aparicio
	Financial services	Jorge Fidalgo
	FMCG, retail	Trinidad Moron
	Manufacturing, engineering	
	Technology	
	Professional services	Carmen Mallagray
Switzerland	Health care, pharmaceuticals	Philipp Buis
	Technology	
	Professional services	Philipp Freyre
	Technology	
	Financial & professional services	Nick Reichstein
	FMCG, retail	Lucas Schellenberg
	Manufacturing, engineering	
UK	Technology	Phil Cray
	Manufacturing, engineering	George Cross
	Financial services	Robert Watsham
	Hospitality, travel	Nicholas Wylde

North America
Canada

Ottawa	Manufacturing, engineering	André Couillard
	Financial services	Arlene Crichton
Toronto	Financial services	Gillian Lansdowne
	Professional services	

US

City	Sector	Name
Atlanta	Manufacturing, engineering	Dean Bare
Austin	Health care, pharmaceuticals	David Harap
Baltimore	CEO, board governance Manufacturing, engineering	H. Edward Muendel
	FMCG, retail Manufacturing, engineering	Steve Cornacchia
	Technology	James Matthews
	Health care, pharmaceuticals	Douglas Norton
Chicago	Financial services	James Piper
	Technology	Jeff Levitt
Dallas	Financial services Resources, energy	Rick Davis
	Professional services	Nancy Keene
	Manufacturing, engineering Resources, energy	Jerry McFarland
	CEO, board governance	Ed Moerbe
	Hospitality, travel	Fred Reed
	Health care, pharmaceuticals	Roger Toney
	Technology	Steve Watson
Denver	Professional services	John Mark
Los Angeles	Technology	Steven Cadwell
	Financial services	Steve Duffy
	Health care, pharmaceuticals Manufacturing, engineering	Edward Savage
Miami	Technology	Robert Beatty
	Hospitality, travel	William Frank
New York	Financial services	Abram Claude Jr
	Technology	James Gladden
	Manufacturing, engineering	Peter Hallock
	Hospitality, travel Technology	Christopher Kull
	CEO, board governance	Andrew Sherwood
	FMCG, retail Health care, pharmaceuticals	Charles Wright
San Francisco	Technology	Reuben Loya
	FMCG, retail Technology	Stacy Holland

Latin America

Argentina/Uruguay	Financial services	Claudio Fernaud
Brazil	FMCG, retail Health care, pharmaceuticals	Eline Kullock
	Financial services Technology	Job Onkenhout
Chile	FMCG, retail Financial services	Ana Maria Krebs
	Hospitality, travel Resources, energy	Carlos Mena
Mexico	Manufacturing, engineering	Jose Brogeras
	FMCG, retail	Gabriela Robles
	Health care, pharmaceuticals	Carmen Suarez

Asia & Australasia

Australia	Financial services	Fiona Lavan
	Manufacturing, engineering Resources, energy	James Allen
	Technology	Robyn Brown
Hong Kong	Technology	Frankie Lam
India		
Bangalore	Technology	Venkatesh Shastry
Chennai	Health care, pharmaceuticals	S. Subburaj
Mumbai	FMCG, retail	Anindita Banerjee
Pune	Manufacturing, engineering	Namrata Thawani
Japan	FMCG, retail Health care, pharmaceuticals	Seiko Ishimoto
	Health care, pharmaceuticals Professional services	Saeko Nagatomi
	Technology CEO, board governance	Minori Shimono
	Professional services Technology	Minako Takeuchi
	Financial services Manufacturing, engineering	Noboru Yamada
South Korea	Health care, pharmaceuticals	Sang-Hoon Han
	FMCG, retail	Janice Kim
	Professional services	So-Jin Kim

Christian & Timbers

Senior management
Chairman and CEO . . . . .Brian M. Sullivan
Chief financial officer/chief operating officer . .David C. Nocifora

Headquarters

North America
570 Lexington Avenue
19th Floor
New York, NY 10022
US
Tel: +1 212 588 3500

Europe
Renoir Christian & Timbers
22 Bedford Square
London WC1B 3HH
UK
Tel: +44 20 7034 1200

Websites
www.ctnet.com
www.renoirct.com

Office locations
Europe   London
North America   Boston, Cleveland, Columbia, Menlo Park, New York,
                Stamford, Tysons Corner

Practice groups
Board of directors
Consumer and retail
Financial services
Life sciences, pharmaceuticals and
  health care

Manufacturing and industrial
Media and entertainment
Technology
Professional services and consulting

Services offered
Executive search

Global performance data

Figures are for 2003 unless stated otherwise

Net revenue	$25.4m[a]
Number of partners	24[b]
Number of researchers	24
Net revenue per consultant	$970,800
Number of offices worldwide	8
% change in net revenue 2003/04	9

a 2004. b Includes consultants.

Global net revenue by industry sector (%)

Board	5
Consumer and retail	4
Financial services	9
Life sciences, pharmaceuticals, health care	8
Manufacturing and industrial	8
Media and entertainment	6
Professional services and consulting	11
Technology	49

Net revenue by geographic region (%)

North America	94
Europe	5
Asia and Australasia	1

Comments

Christian & Timbers was established in 1980 and the firm has built a reputation as a premium recruiter in the technology and telecommunications fields. Clients include high-profile early-stage companies through to the *Fortune* Global 500.

The firm is now expanding its capabilities in other sectors such as financial services, life sciences, consumer, and media and entertainment by recruiting more consultants. For example, Brenda Burnett-Stohner and Burke St John, who were both among the top-ten producing consultants at Heidrick & Struggles, have now joined Christian & Timbers.

It is a medium-sized executive search firm with seven offices in the United States and an affiliation in the UK with a boutique firm, Renoir (Renoir Christian & Timbers). Renoir's expertise is primarily in technology and financial services.

Brian Sullivan, who was formerly a vice-chairman of Heidrick &

Struggles, became CEO of Christian & Timbers in September 2004. He is embarking on a strategy to broaden the firm's industry specialisation and to expand the firm's capabilities beyond the United States.

Sectors and specialists

E-mail address format varies.

US	Sector	Consultant
Boston	Board services CEOs Industrial, manufacturing Information technology Private equity, venture capital	Stephen P. Mader
	Electronic manufacturing services Enterprise software Health care Professional services Telecommunications Board services	Robert M. Nephew
	Emerging technologies Enterprise software IT services Life sciences	Leonard A. Vairo
	Enterprise software Professional services Telecommunications	Jeff M. Leopold
	Consumer products Financial services Professional services Software Venture capital	David J. Merwin
	Enterprise software Internet security Manufacturing Software infrastructure Telecommunications	Jennifer M. Condon
	Enterprise software Information technology Life sciences Semiconductors Telecommunications	Peter Dube

Cleveland	Computer software Consulting services Engineering, environmental, energy services Manufacturing Private equity firms Venture capital	Adam P. Kohn
	Board services Industrial Information technology International Operations Professional services	Umesh Ramakrishnan
	Semiconductor Wireless	Christopher J. Conti
	Legal Semiconductor, electronics	Joshua B. Nathanson
	Manufacturing Professional services Software	John K. Westropp
	Software Venture capital	James C. Carter
	Financial services Information technology Professional services Retail, business distribution	Robert F. Voth
	Board services Consumer products Education, training, e-learning Life sciences	Gregory J. Lovas
	Electronics Semiconductor Software Venture capital	Bradley R. Westveld
Columbia	Board services Education Semiconductor, applied technology Software Telecommunications	Buster M. Houchins Jr

	Life sciences Semiconductor, high-tech instruments	Ernest W. Brittingham
	Life sciences Medical devices Semiconductor, electronics Software	Stacy A. Braun
Menlo Park	Board services Enterprise computing Networking, communications	Craig G. Smith
	Board services Software Telecom Venture capital Wireless	Robert L. Forman
	Enterprise software	Simon J. Francis
	Communications Early-stage, venture-backed Enterprise software Fortune 500	Lexi A. Slavet
New York	Media, entertainment Technology	Paula A. Seibel
	Professional services Managed client services Business, information services	Adam J. Prager
	Digital media Enterprise software Games Publishing Web services	Andrew C. LaValle
	Semiconductor Software Storage Venture capital	Jeffrey I. Shapiro
	Professional services Software	Marc Gasperino
Stamford	Computer software, hardware E-commerce New media Systems integration, IT services	John C. Daily

	Asset management	Mark A. Esposito
	Capital markets	
	Commercial banking	
	Consumer finance	
	Financial e-commerce	
	Insurance	
	Venture capital	
	Asset management	Glenn M. Buggy
	Financial services	
	Hedge funds	
	Insurance	
	Legal, professional services	
	Private equity	
	Wealth management	
Tysons Corner	Board services	Kerry D. Moynihan
	For-profit education	
	Private equity firms	
	(IPO, venture capital)	
	Technology	
	Transaction processing	
	Advanced technology	Martin Mendelsohn
	Corporate security	
	Federal solutions	
	Private equity	
	Professional services	
	Consumer goods	Richard W. Herman
	Financial services	
	Software	
	Technology	

UK

Renoir C&T, London	Communications	Marc Lenot
	Semiconductor	Adam Bloch
	Software, services	Thomas Jepsen
	Technology	Ben Anderson

Eric Salmon & Partners

Senior management

Chairman . . . . Eric Salmon
CEO . . . . Christian Lanis

Partners

François Barbier	Eric Salmon
Didier Duval	Gert Schmidt
Christian Lanis	Aileen Taylor
Massimo Milletti	Hans Thoenes
Fabrizio Panzeri	Sophie Wigniolle

Headquarters

144 Avenue des Champs-Elysées
75008 Paris
France
Tel: +33 1 7275 2525

Website

www.ericsalmon.com

Office locations

Europe	Frankfurt, London, Milan, Paris
Americas	New York

Practice groups

Automotive and industrial	Foundations and not-for-profit
Boards and non-executive directors	Luxury goods
Consumer and retail	Pharmaceuticals and health care
Energy	Professional services and consulting
Financial services	Technology

Services offered

Executive search	Management audit

Global performance data

Figures are for 2004

Net revenue	$16m
Number of consultants	18
Number of researchers	13
Net revenue per consultant	$694,444
Number of offices worldwide	5
% change in net revenue 2003/04	28

Global net revenue by industry sector (%)

Consumer, retail, luxury	30
Financial services	10
Pharmaceuticals, health care, biotechnology	10
Automotive, industrial	25
Boards, non-executive directors	10
Professional services, consulting	5
Technology	10

Global net revenue by function (%)

Chairman, CEO, board directors	20
Non-executive directors	10
Financial	20
IT/technology	10
Human resources	15
Legal	5
Marketing and sales	20

Net revenue by geographic region (%)

Europe, Middle East & Africa	90
North America	10

Comments

Eric Salmon & Partners was founded simultaneously in Paris and Milan in 1990 by Eric Salmon, who adopted many of the principles that governed Egon Zehnder where he had previously worked. The company is owned by its partners and has five offices in Paris, Milan, Frankfurt, London and New York. Although he handed over day-to-day management of the firm in 2004, Eric Salmon remains an active and widely regarded consultant, especially in European CEO searches.

The 18 consultants, who reflect the firm's pan-European nature, work

185

as one global team with a cross-border approach. Given the size of the firm there is a strong team culture. The majority of its assignments are multicountry and often include countries where the firm does not have an office. Conducting these assignments is made easier by the one-firm partnership model and the absence of any disputes over fee allocation.

Eric Salmon boasts a high level of repeat business and completion ratios above the industry average, and it plans to focus on what it knows best. This is likely to include the strengthening of existing offices rather than the opening of new ones. Frankfurt and London, which are smaller than the Paris and Milan offices, will seek to recruit additional consultants to strengthen the firm's presence in these markets.

Although the firm does not operate a strict industry practice structure its consultants generally operate in one sector (where they may do 70–80% of their work), but they also conduct assignments in other areas. Traditionally, the firm's strengths have been in the industrial, automotive and consumer and luxury goods sectors, but it is also strong in health care, professional and financial services, and technology. The firm is good at cross-border search because most of the consultants are multilingual and have multicountry experience.

The management assessment business has grown out of existing client relationships. Non-executive director work is also an increasingly important part of the business.

Sectors and specialists

E-mail address format varies.

Europe	Sector	Consultant
France	Automotive	Jean-Pierre Bellingard
	Industry	Didier Duval
		Eric Salmon
	Consumer	Yves Delloye
		Christian Lanis
	Financial services	Sophie Wigniolle
	Health care	Laurence Viénot
	Professional services	Anne Romet
	Technology	Didier Duval
Germany	Automotive	Gert Schmidt
	Consumer	
	Industry	
	Technology	

	Consumer Industry	Francois Barbier
	Health care	Claudia Schutz
Italy	Automotive Industry	Massimo Milletti Hans Thoenes
	Consumer Technology	Alessandra Agnoletto
	Financial & professional services	Fabrizio Panzeri
	Professional services	Alessandro Molinaroli
UK	Consumer (luxury goods) Retail	Aileen Taylor
	Professional services Technology	Anthony Harling

North America

US	Automotive Industry Financial services Professional services	Fabrizio Panzeri

Penrhyn International

Senior management

Chairman ....Skott B. Burkland
Europe ....Anders H. Borg
UK ....Christopher Mill
Australia ....Paul Bennett

Headquarters

North America
8 Ranney Hill Road
Morristown, NJ 07960
US
Tel: +1 973 644 0900

Europe
205 Rue Belliard
1040 Brussels
Belgium
Tel: +32 2 2310635

Website

www.penrhyn.com

Office locations

Europe	Brussels, Dusseldorf, Hamburg, London, Madrid, Munich, Paris, Stockholm, Zurich
Americas	Buenos Aires, Chicago, New York, San Francisco, Santiago, São Paulo
Asia & Australasia	Melbourne, Mumbai, Tokyo

Practice groups

Automotive and industrial
Boards and non-executive directors
Consumer and retail
Energy
Financial services
Foundations and not-for-profit

Pharmaceuticals and health care
 (life sciences)
Professional services and consulting
Technology, communications
 and media
Logistics

Services offered

Executive search
Management audit

Succession planning

Global performance data

Figures are for 2004

Net revenue	$15m
Number of partners	45[a]
Number of researchers	42
Net revenue per consultant	$334,000
Number of offices worldwide	18
% change in net revenue 2003/04	n/a

a Includes consultants.

Comments

Founded in 1979 in Brussels, Penrhyn now has 18 offices worldwide and is a federation of search firms. Member firms often work together, and the Penrhyn identity is increasingly being enhanced as they co-operate on cross-border projects. Although the group has grown steadily, it is eager to emphasise that shared values and practice standards take priority over rapid geographic expansion.

The firm is particularly well known for its work in IT, with strong practices in London (Christopher Mill), Brussels (Hansar), Zurich (Hitchman), Munich (Lachner, Aden, Beyer), Mumbai (3P), Tokyo (Shimamoto), and Melbourne and Sydney (Fish & Nankivell, Ogilvie, Watson). Plans for adding North American technology expertise are in progress. Skott/Edwards in New York specialises in biotechnology and life sciences.

Strengths in Europe include cross-border practices in Brussels in life sciences, consumer goods and financial and professional services (Hansar International) and in London in professional services (Christopher Mill & Partners). In Asia, Shimamoto Partners in Tokyo is known for its medical, pharmaceutical and financial services practices, and in Mumbai 3P has concentrations in manufacturing and services.

Opportunities for growth are likely to come from Europe and Asia and from increased technology business in the United States as they strengthen their presence there.

Sectors and specialists

E-mail address format varies.

Europe	Sector	Name
Belgium	Automotive, industry Media, entertainment	Clare Ireland
	Consumer Health care Professional services Legal & government affairs Technology	Anders Borg
	Financial services	Sonja Hickl-Szabo
France	Automotive, industry Consumer Media, entertainment	Guy Lang
	Commodities, trading Energy, oil Financial services	Jean Richard Finot
	Financial services Middle East, North Africa	Martin Boyer
Germany	Automotive, industry Media, entertainment	Peter Lachner
	Energy, oil Public sector Utilities	Klaus Aden
	Health care	Fritz Gruppe
	Professional services Technology	Frank Beyer
Spain	Consumer Health care Technology	Luis Truchado
	Financial services Professional services	Francisco Martin
Switzerland	Automotive, industry Financial services Media, entertainment	Roy Hitchman
	Consumer	Peter Forster
	Professional services Technology	Urs Keim

Sweden	Automotive, industry Media, entertainment	Clare Ireland
	Consumer Health care Legal & government affairs Professional services Technology	Anders Borg
	Financial services	Sonja Hickl-Szabo
UK	Automotive, industry	Mike Stein
	Consumer Financial services	John Salmon
	Financial services Legal	David Goldstone
	Automotive, industry Professional services Technology	Christopher Mill

North America

US	Automotive, industry Financial services Media, entertainment	Jack Clarey
	Consumer Professional services	Greg Klein
	Biotechnology Health care	Skott Burkland

Latin America

Brazil	Consumer Health care Legal	Paula Sampaio
Chile	Consumer	Andres Undurraga
	Financial services	Rafael Rodriguez
Argentina	Automotive, industry Professional services	Daniel Feraud
	Consumer Media, entertainment	Roberto Vola-Luhrs
	Energy, oil Health care	Ricardo Mayer
	Technology	Jorge Berman

Asia & Australasia

Australia	Automotive, industry	Ian Nankivell
	Financial services	
	Health care	
	Media, entertainment	
	Automotive, industry	Richard Ogilvie
	Consumer	
	Energy, oil	
	Professional services	Phil Watson
	Technology	Paul Bennett
	Education, government	Kathy McLean
Japan	Consumer	Casey Shimamoto
	Professional services	
	Technology	
	Financial services	Yuhiko Yasunaga
	Retail	
India	Automotive, industry	Nirmit Parekh
	Consumer	
	Financial services	Raju Kapoor
	Professional services	
	Technology	
	Health care	Mitchelle Shetty

ITP Worldwide

Senior management

Chairman . . . . .R. Paul Kors
Vice-chairman . . . . .Europe: Etienne Reeners
Asia Pacific: Theresa Goh

Board of directors

Charles Polachi
Etienne Reeners
Theresa Goh
Eric Dieny

John Kato
Andrew Price
R. Paul Kors

Headquarters

North America
Kors Montgomery International/
ITP Worldwide
14811 St Mary's Lane, Suite 280
Houston, TX 77079
US
Tel: +1 713 849 7101

Europe
Hightech Partners/ITP Worldwide
Avenue Louise 479/58
1050 Brussels
Belgium
Tel: +32 2 663 1600

Asia
Resource Dynamics/ITP Worldwide
133 Cecil Street
Keck Sing Tower 17-03
Singapore 069535
Tel: +65 6626 6460

Website

www.itpww.com

Office locations

Europe	Brussels, Copenhagen, Frankfurt, London, Oslo, Paris
Americas	Boston, Houston, Los Angeles, San Diego, Silicon Valley, Toronto
Asia & Australasia	Auckland, Bangalore, Chennai, Hong Kong, Shanghai, Singapore, Sydney, Taipei, Tokyo

Practice groups
Technology executive search (95% of revenue)
Management assessment (2% of revenue)

Services offered
Executive search
Management audit, executive assessment

Global performance data
Figures are for 2003 unless stated otherwise

Net revenue	$14m[a]
Number of partners	22
Number of researchers	18[b]
Net revenue per consultant	$636,400
Number of offices worldwide	21
% change in net revenue 2003/04	16.6

a 2004. b Includes consultants.

Global net revenue by industry sector (%)

Biopharmaceuticals	4
Technology	95
of which:	
– communications	7
– computer systems	7
– consulting & systems	10
– corporate IT	2
– content & media	5
– networking	6
– semiconductor	10
– software	28
– storage	7
– venture capital & private equity	6
– wireless	7

Global net revenue by function (%)

CEO, president, board directors	9
VC & private equity partners	4
CFO, finance	11
CIO, internal IS	8
General management	15
Engineering	6
Human resources	3
Marketing	11
Professional services	3
Sales	25
Research and development	5

Net revenue by geographic region (%)

North America	52
Asia Pacific	31
Europe	16
Latin America	1

Comments

ITP (International Technology Partners) was founded in 1993 in Lexington, Massachusetts, by three American and one European search firms specialising in technology. The firms were Fenwick Partners (now Polachi & Co), Hightech Partners, Kors Montgomery International and Schweichler Associates (now Schweichler, Price & Partners). The firm now has 11 shareholder member firms and 21 offices including all of the original partners.

The firm still focuses on technology and 95% of its global search revenue comes from this sector. A requirement for membership of ITP is that a firm must be one of the top three independent technology executive search firms in its market. ITP believes that it is the only technology-focused executive search group operating on a worldwide basis – it is essentially a global boutique. As such, it claims to provide a uniform service to technology companies around the world with the advantages of a local independent firm.

ITP has members in 16 countries. In the United States member firms are well respected for recruiting CEOs and other C-level executives (such as CFOs) for venture-capital-funded companies in their early stages. In Europe and Asia, the group is known for finding executives to run local and regional operations of American, European and

Japanese companies. In Japan, where it works for both Japanese and western companies, ITP is one of only three Japanese-owned firms that work on a retainer basis (others work on a contingency basis).

The continuing recovery of the technology sector represents a good opportunity for ITP, but its reputation is still based on that of its individual members rather than ITP Worldwide, and its challenge is to become better known as a global firm with huge expertise in the technology sector.

Sectors and specialists

All consultants are technology generalists who work with companies ranging from venture-capital-backed start-ups to multinational firms. Areas of work include software, storage, semiconductors, hardware, communications, outsourcing and systems integration.
E-mail address format varies.

Europe	Company	Consultant
Belgium	Hightech Partners, Brussels	Etienne Reeners
Denmark	Hightech Partners, Copenhagen	Michael Storm
France	Hightech Partners, Paris	Dominique Moracchini
Germany	Hightech Partners, Frankfurt	Edmund Bernardi
UK	Hightech Partners, London	Dilip Chandra

North America	Company	Consultant
Canada	Stratum Executive Search, Toronto	Patrick Galpin
US	Polachi & Company, Sherborn	Hale Cochran
		Paul Moran
		Jim Poe
		Charles Polachi
		Peter Polachi
		Doug Rothstein
		Maura McShane
	Schweichler, Price & Partners, Larkspur	Dave Mularkey
		Andy Price
		Lee Schweichler
	Kors Montgomery, Houston	R. Paul Kors

Asia & Australasia

Australia	JSP Associates, Sydney	John Price
Japan	TESCO, Tokyo	John Kato
		Ted Oiwa
Singapore	Resource Dynamics, Singapore	Theresa Goh
		Ken Leow
India	Quorum Group, Mumbai/ Bangalore	Arum Mani
New Zealand	Fleet Partners, Auckland	Barry Dreyer
China	EMS	Eric Dieny
Taiwan	Shanghai, Taipei	Olivier Roy

Boyden

Senior management

Chairman . . . . .Fred Greene
President . . . . .Christopher Clarke

Directors

Americas . . . . .Trina Gordon
Europe, Middle East and Africa . . .Marc Lamy, Pasi Koivusaari,
Wolfgang Bersch, Jaime Ferrer
Asia Pacific . . . . .Dinesh Mirchandani

Headquarters

364 Elwood Avenue
Hawthorne
New York, NY 10532
US
Tel: +1 914 747 0093

Website

www.boyden.com

Office locations

(Some cities have more than one office)

Europe	Amsterdam, Athens, Barcelona, Brussels, Budapest, Copenhagen, Dublin, Dusseldorf, Frankfurt/Bad Homburg, Helsinki, Istanbul, Lisbon, London, Madrid, Milan, Moscow, Munich, Oslo, Paris, Prague, Rome, St Petersburg, Stockholm, Valencia, Warsaw, Zurich
Americas	Atlanta, Baltimore, Bogota, Buenos Aires, Calgary, Caracas, Chicago, Detroit, Houston, Lima, Mexico City, New York, Phoenix, Pittsburgh, San Francisco, St Louis, Santiago, São Paulo, Summit, Toronto, Washington DC
Asia & Australasia	Auckland, Bangalore, Bangkok, Beijing, Guangzhou, Hong Kong, Jakarta, Kuala Lumpur, Manila, Melbourne, Mumbai, Pune, Seoul, Shanghai, Singapore, Sydney, Taipei, Tokyo
Middle East & Africa	Johannesburg

Practice groups

Board search

Board effectiveness evaluation
Corporate governance

Development of a model board
Recruitment for boards

Consumer products

Advertising
Apparel
Consumer durable goods
Consumer packaged goods
Food and beverage

Leisure
Luxury goods
Media and entertainment
Retail
Travel and hospitality

Financial services

Asset management
Brokerage
Commercial finance
Corporate banking
Corporate finance and
  capital markets
Fundamental, technical and
  quantitative research
Insurance
Investor services
Leasing
Mergers and acquisitions

Outsourcing and management control
Payments
Portfolio management
Private client services
Private equity/venture capital
Private wealth management
Real estate
Retail banking
Risk management
Structured finance
Treasury services

Industrial

Agriculture
Automotive
Aviation
Chemical
Construction
Defence

Energy
Manufacturing
Mining and metals
Packaging and forest products
Transportation and logistics
Utilities

Life sciences and health care

Animal health; distribution
Biotechnology
Health information products
  and services

Health-care providers
Medical devices and supplies
Pharmaceuticals

Speciality

Diversity	Industrial security/strategic
Education	risk management
Generalist	Interim management
Government	Not-for-profit
Human resources	Professional services

Technology

Communications	Outsourcing
Emerging technologies	Professional and IT services
Internet services	Semiconductors and electronics
Networking	Systems and software
New media	

Services offered

Executive search	Interim management
Management assessment	Management consulting
Executive coaching	

Global performance data

Figures are for 2004

Net revenue	n/a
Number of partners	214[a]
Number of researchers	133
Net revenue per consultant	n/a
Number of offices worldwide	69
% change in net revenue 2003/04	n/a

a Billing associates.

Comments

Boyden was founded by Sidney Boyden in 1946 and is the oldest of the major international firms. It was a pioneer in executive search in the days when the idea of paying someone to find leaders was new. Major consulting firms such as McKinsey and Booz Allen Hamilton had been advising their clients on leadership, and this was what Sidney Boyden was doing at Booz Allen before he founded his own firm to serve this need. Between 1946 and 1970, Sidney Boyden built the largest search firm in the world and then sold the business and retired. In the recession of the early 1990s, Boyden downsized and other search firms overtook it in terms of size.

omotive, industry	Bruce Abbott
rgy, oil	
sumer	Rebecca Willet
ncial services	David Richard
lth care	Graeme Rogers
ia, entertainment	Julie M. Bayliss
essional services	Carl Baverstock
nology	
sumer	Yukio Soeda
nology	
ncial services	Yujiro Miyake
essional services	Yoshiyuki Okamoto
sumer	Dinesh Mirchandani
essional services	
nology	
ncial services	Ashok Ghia

Since 2000 Boyden has been making great strides with offices in all major markets, and the firm is now well placed in emerging markets too. It offers executive search and interim management, management assessment and related management consulting services. Boyden's organisational structure is similar to that of the major accounting firms, with local ownership of each office by the local partners and the worldwide company and the brand owned by its senior search consultants/partners. This means that it does not have to worry about external shareholders and the partners have a sense of professional freedom. However, decisions on how the firm is run require considerable discussion among the senior partners and radical changes can be difficult to achieve. Furthermore, local ownership can cause problems of loyalty in cross-border searches.

Boyden is especially strong in financial services, manufacturing and high technology. It also has well-established groups in life sciences, consumer products, human resources and not-for-profit. The firm is increasingly working in niche areas such as mining and oil and gas. Boyden is growing its interim management business, especially in the UK and France, and its board search practice.

Boyden sees the biggest opportunities ahead in the growth of directorship searches as a result of the tightening of regulations, the retirement of many directors and the reshaping of boards. Chris Clarke says:

> [We see search] moving towards a true profession. [There needs to be] more careful screening of search firms' own candidates: in recent years some search firms found that some of their leaders and even their CEOs had falsified their own CVs or been involved in unethical or fraudulent behaviour. Firms must have higher entry standards, rigorous training, quality control procedures and the highest ethics.

Since 2000 Boyden has been making great strides with offices in all major markets, and the firm is now well placed in emerging markets too. It offers executive search and interim management, management assessment and related management consulting services. Boyden's organisational structure is similar to that of the major accounting firms, with local ownership of each office by the local partners and the world-wide company and the brand owned by its senior search consultants/partners. This means that it does not have to worry about external shareholders and the partners have a sense of professional freedom. However, decisions on how the firm is run require considerable discussion among the senior partners and radical changes can be difficult to achieve. Furthermore, local ownership can cause problems of loyalty in cross-border searches.

Boyden is especially strong in financial services, manufacturing and high technology. It also has well-established groups in life sciences, consumer products, human resources and not-for-profit. The firm is increasingly working in niche areas such as mining and oil and gas. Boyden is growing its interim management business, especially in the UK and France, and its board search practice.

Boyden sees the biggest opportunities ahead in the growth of directorship searches as a result of the tightening of regulations, the retirement of many directors and the reshaping of boards. Chris Clarke says:

> [We see search] moving towards a true profession. [There needs to be] more careful screening of search firms' own candidates: in recent years some search firms found that some of their leaders and even their CEOs had falsified their own CVs or been involved in unethical or fraudulent behaviour. Firms must have higher entry standards, rigorous training, quality control procedures and the highest ethics.

Sectors and specialists

E-mail address format varies.

Europe	*Sector*	*Consultant*
Belgium	Automotive, industry	Jac Van Den Broek
	Energy, oil	
	Consumer	
	Financial services	
	Health care	
	Technology	Leendert van den Beukel
Denmark	Consumer	Soren Mejer Johansen
	Financial services	
	Professional services	Olav Kieler
	Health care	Jens Otto Tram
	Technology	Kenneth Mortensen
France	Automotive, industry	Charles-Antoine de Gastines
	Life sciences	Michel Sauzay
	Board services	Marc Lamy
		Michel Sauzay
	Consumer	Marc Julienne
		Marie-Pierre Guilbert
	Energy, oil	Robert A. Bell
	Financial services	Marc Lamy
		Antoine Kamphuis
	Interim management	Gérard Fournier
	Media, entertainment	Gérard Fournier
	Professional services	Frédéric d'Antin
	Technology	Eymeric Prot
Germany	Automotive, industry	Gerhard J. Raisig
	Consumer	Wolfgang Bersch
	Energy, oil	Dominik von Winterfeldt
	Financial services	Dieter Bleise
	Health care	Werner Schwab
	Media, entertainment	Richard Fudickar
	Professional services	Thomas Breitzmann
	Technology	Michael Kerber
Italy	Automotive, industry	Nicola G. da Vinci
	Consumer	Antonio Cellè
	Energy, oil	Giuseppe Campellone
	Financial services	Siro Bassani
	Health care	Patrizia Bomba

	Media, entertainment	Filippo Pugliese
	Professional services	Sandro Ciani
	Technology	Roberto Delconte
Netherlands	Consumer	Aris Begemann
	Financial services	Peter Hendriks
	Professional services	George Sanne
Spain	Automotive, industry	Jaime Ferrer
	Consumer	Jean F. Berenguer
	Energy, oil	Miguel Angel Tarrés
	Financial services	José E. Sánchez Montalar
	Media, entertainment	Fernando Torras
	Technology	Alfredo Canal
Switzerland	Financial services	Evelyne Thalmann
	Professional services	
	Technology	Rolf Leimer
UK	Automotive, industry	Alan Stamper
	Consumer	Tony McManus
	Financial services	Cathy Holley
	Media, entertainment	Lisa Hobbs
	Professional services	Lisa Gerhardt
	Technology	John Ellis

North America

Canada	Energy, oil	Donna McNeely
	Financial services	
	Media, entertainment	
	Technology	G. Michael Wolkensperg
US	Automotive, industry	E. Wade Close Jr
	Consumer	Meredith Moore
	Energy, oil	Charles A. Rhoads
	Financial services	Jeanne E. Branthover
	Health care	Steve Kane
	Media, entertainment	Mai Keklak
	Professional services	Daniel J. Carney
	Technology	Matthew J. Vossler

Asia & Australasia

Australia	Automotive, industry	Bruce Abbott
	Energy, oil	
	Consumer	Rebecca Willet
	Financial services	David Richard
	Health care	Graeme Rogers
	Media, entertainment	Julie M. Bayliss
	Professional services	Carl Baverstock
	Technology	
Japan	Consumer	Yukio Soeda
	Technology	
	Financial services	Yujiro Miyake
	Professional services	Yoshiyuki Okamoto
India	Consumer	Dinesh Mirchandani
	Professional services	
	Technology	
	Financial services	Ashok Ghia

5 Sector specialists: leading consultants and boutiques

The executive search market is consolidating into large global firms – which offer a well-known brand name, many sectors of industry expertise, and a geographic presence in most markets – and the smaller, well-positioned boutiques – which specialise in the sectors in which they operate. Sector specialists who work within the global firms and boutique specialists claim that they are dedicated, relationship-oriented and client-focused with tailor-made solutions. So how do you decide which consultant and which firm to select?

- **Reputation.** The reputation of the firm in the sector is crucial. How many assignments has it successfully completed in the sector? What is its strength and reputation within your key markets? For example, the Calgary member of a network's energy practice group may be highly regarded, but the group may not be well represented in Houston, London or elsewhere. Integrated firms should monitor their standards worldwide, but this is not always the case.
- **Relationship with competitors.** How many of your firm's competitors does the headhunter currently work for? If the number is high, many of these firms will be off-limits as hunting grounds and this could severely limit the potential pool of candidates.
- **Personal chemistry.** As well as getting on with the headhunter, you need someone who understands the key drivers of the position, your corporate culture and is responsive to your requirements.
- **Strength of market intelligence.** For example, how well do the team members know the key players in your field, and how likely is it that a key player will respond to their calls?

This chapter contains a listing by sector of specialised boutiques and key individual consultants who run practice groups within the leading global firms.

Although financial services has traditionally been the largest sector of business for search firms, the industrial, consumer and technology

Table 5.1 Percentage revenue by industry sector for leading firms[ab]

	Consumer goods, retail	Energy, oil, natural resources[c]	Not-for-profit, education, public sector	Financial services	Industrial, manufacturing, energy, oil, automotive	Life sciences, health care, pharmaceuticals, biotechnology	Media, entertainment	Professional services	Technology, telecoms	Other
A.T. Kearney	13	–	15	16	19	14	–	4	19	–
Christian & Timbers	4	–	–	9	8	8	6	11	49	5
Eric Salmon	30	–	–	10	25	10	–	5	10	10
Globe	27	–	6	12	19	13	–	11	12	–
Heidrick	16	–	3	28	20	9	–	9	15	–
Highland	16	–	–	32	15	19	–	9	9	–
ITP	–	–	–	–	–	4	–	–	95	–
Korn/Ferry	23	–	5	15	23	15	–	–	18	1
Ray & Berndtson	13	–	–	13	15	8	–	5	8	38
Russell Reynolds	15	–	–	28	22	10	–	–	25	–
Signium	10	2	1	5	32	8	–	20	17	5
Spencer Stuart	17	7	2	19	16	14	–	7	17	1
Stanton Chase	13	5	–	19	23	9	–	8	17	7
Whitehead Mann	17	–	8	45	12	4	–	6	8[d]	–

Note: may not indicate zero; this category may be included elsewhere.
a Not all firms collect or divulge these data.
b Totals may not add to 100% because of rounding.
c Where separated out from the industrial sector.
d Includes media.

Table 5.2 **Industry sectors as a percentage of total search business**

Sector	%[a]
Financial services	21
Industrial, manufacturing, automotive, energy, oil	19
Consumer goods, retail	17
Technology, telecoms	17
Life sciences, health care, pharmaceuticals, biotechnology	11
Professional services	5
Not-for-profit, education, public sector	3
Energy, oil, natural resources[b]	1

a Based on revenues and percentage breakdowns provided by 14 of the 20 leading global firms as detailed in profiles in Chapter 4 and Table 5.1.
b Where reported separately from industrial sector.

sectors are catching up. Between them these first four sectors (financial services, industrial, consumer and technology) represent around 75% of total assignments for the largest search firms. The life sciences sector is steadily growing, especially in the biotechnology field. Not-for-profit, public sector, education are also growing, particularly in the United States and the UK. Data for the media and entertainment sector, which headhunters report is another growing area, are often included in the consumer or technology sectors.

Note that not all firms have practice groups in all sectors; firms profiled in Chapter 4 may have specialists.

Automotive, industrial, manufacturing

The automotive sector divides into original equipment and suppliers. There are specialist headhunters who know Ford, GM, Chrysler, Toyota and so on and those who know the various parts makers around the world. The industrial and manufacturing sector covers companies involved in the manufacture of components, parts and finished goods, and in the fabrication of metals, plastics and other raw materials. It also covers capital equipment companies, transport components and other durables. Also in this sector are the agricultural products, engineering and construction, wholesaling and distribution, paper and chemicals industries. Most of the specialists are part of large global firms. In the United States the heart of the sector is in the midwest, and in Europe it is in the UK and Germany.

Boutiques

Company	Location	Consultant	Website
CareerSmith (construction)	Newport Beach	Brian Smith	www.careersmith.com
Nedelcu & Company (automotive)	Munich	Jon Nedelcu	n/a

Global firms' practice leaders

Company	Location	Consultant
Amrop Hever	Hamburg	Ulrich Dade
A.T. Kearney	Fort Worth	Paul Ray Jr
Boyden	Detroit; St Louis	Denis Sullivan (automotive); George Zamborsky (industry)
Egon Zehnder	Berlin	Jörg Ritter
Eric Salmon	Frankfurt; Milan	Gert Schmidt; Massimo Milletti
Globe Search	London	Guy Beresford
Heidrick & Struggles	Chicago	Dale M. Visokey
Highland Partners	Dallas	James M. Bethmann
IIC Partners	Sydney; Hong Kong	Kris de Jager (automotive); Ivo A. Hahn (industrial)
Korn/Ferry	Chicago	Scott E. Kingdom
Ray & Berndtson	New York	Tracy O'Such
Russell Reynolds	Houston; New York; Paris	John Freud; William Henderson; Christophe Tellier
Spencer Stuart	Chicago	Bob Heidrick
Stanton Chase	Baltimore	Steve Cornacchia
Transearch	Paris	Christian de Charette
Whitehead Mann	London	Paul Turner

Consumer, retail, luxury goods

This sector includes fast-moving consumer goods (FMCG), consumer services, consumer internet, luxury and branded apparel, retail, leisure and hospitality. It also usually extends to cover entertainment and sports management. The sector is served by a mixture of boutique firms and specialists in the global firms. In the United States, Herbert Mines is a highly regarded boutique in consumer, retail and fashion as are Kirk Palmer and Kenzer Corporation.

Boutiques

Company	Location	Consultant	Website
Bó Lè	Hong Kong	Louisa Rousseau	www.bole.com
Gould McCoy Chadick & Ellig	New York	Millington McCoy	www.gmcsearch.com
Gow & Partners	London; Warsaw; New York; Hong Kong	Roddy Gow	www.gowpartners.com
Herbert Mines/ Globe	New York	Herbert Reiter	www.herbertmines.com
Kenzer Corporation	New York	Robert Kenzer	www.kenzer.com
Kirk Palmer	New York	Kirk Palmer	www.kirkpalmer.com
Search Partners International	Paris	Roberto Valagussa	www.searchpartners.it

Global firms' practice leaders

Company	Location	Consultant
Amrop Hever	Amsterdam	Andrew J. Rommes
A.T. Kearney	Chicago	Robert Tate
Boyden	Atlanta	Dave Gallagher
Egon Zehnder	New York	Justus John O'Brien
Eric Salmon	London; Paris	Aileen Taylor; Christian Lanis
Globe Search	London; New York	Nigel Smith & Chris Stainton; Harold Reiter
Heidrick & Struggles	Madrid	Eduardo Antunovic
Highland Partners	Atlanta	Bud Wright
Korn/Ferry	Chicago	Tierney Remick
Ray & Berndtson	London	Laurence Vallaeys
Russell Reynolds	Paris	Henry de Montebello
Spencer Stuart	Chicago	Joseph Kopsick
Stanton Chase	Amsterdam	Peter de Jong
Transearch	Hong Kong	Vincent Swift
Whitehead Mann	London	Carol Leonard

Energy, oil, natural resources

This sector covers firms that specialise in oil and gas exploration and production, refining and marketing, and the mining of natural resources. Utilities is a particular growth area, as are smaller sectors such as environmental services and technical professionals within exploration and exploitation. The liberalisation of energy markets in Europe has resulted in a broad range of recruitment needs, and evolving sectors such as LNG (liquid natural gas) and renewables such as wind and wave are becoming increasingly relevant job opportunity areas. There are a number of specialised boutique firms operating in this sector, mainly based in centres such as London, Houston and Moscow.

The sector is well served by the global firms too; for example, Russell Reynolds has an energy practice group as do many of the other large firms.

Boutiques

Company	Location	Consultant	Website
cFour Partners	Houston	R. Paul Kors	www.itpww.com
Cordiner King Hever	Melbourne	Richard King	www.amrophever.com
Cripps Sears	London	Michael Cripps	www.crippssears.com
Curzon Partners	London	Lachlan Rhodes	www.curzonpartnership.com
Preng & Co	Houston; London; Moscow	David Preng	www.preng.com

Global firms' practice leaders

Company	Location	Consultant
A.T. Kearney	Dusseldorf	Martin Schubert
Boyden	Houston	James Hertlein
Heidrick & Struggles	Houston	Andrew W. Talkington
Eric Salmon	Frankfurt	François Barbier
IIC Partners	London	Lachlan Rhodes
Korn/Ferry	Houston	John McKay, Richard Preng
Russell Reynolds	London	Mat Green
Stanton Chase	Dallas	Jerry McFarland
Transearch	Toronto	Russ Buckland

Financial services

The financial services sector is the largest speciality sector in Europe and constitutes roughly 50% of assignments in the region for most of the global firms. The UK is the predominant market followed by Germany. Key financial centres dominate the business and concentrations of boutiques exist in New York, London and Hong Kong. There are many specialist boutique firms that can be divided into the following five subsectors:

- consumer financial services
- global banking and markets (investment banking)
- investment management
- insurance
- real estate

Venture capital and start-ups are also often considered as a separate sector within financial services and have dedicated search specialists as are legal, HR and private equity.

Boutiques

Company	Location	Consultant	Website
Europe			
33 St James's	London	Bruce Beringer	www.33stjamess.com
Alexander Mann	London	Mike Brennan	www.alexmann.com
Armstrong International	London	Martin Armstrong	www.armstrongint.com
Bao & Partners	Madrid	Richard Taunton	www.baopartners.com
Blackwood up	London	Susie Cummings	www.blackwoodgroup.com
Cinven	London	Tim Macready	www.skillcapital.com
Gow & Partners	London; Warsaw; New York; Hong Kong	Roddy Gow	www.gowpartners.com
CV Financial Executive Search	Stockholm	Ulrik Swedrup	www.cvsearch.se
Hanover Search	London	Susan Stayne Jackson	www.hanover-search.com
Harvey Nash	London	David Higgens	www.harveynash.com
Hogarth Davies Lloyd	London	Guy Davies James Hogarth	www.hogarthdavieslloyd.com
Hoggett Bowers	London	Petra Rickmeyer	www.hoggett-bowers.co.uk
Longbridge International	London	Frank Varela	www.longbridge.com
Michael Page	London	Jonathan Williams	www.michaelpage.com
Rose Partnership	London	Philippa Rose	www.rosepartnership.com
Sainty Hird	London	Julian Sainty	www.saintyhird.com

| Whitney Group | London | Gary Goldstein | www.whitneygroup.com |
| Singer Hamilton | Paris | Eric Singer | www.singerhamilton.com |

Americas

Armstrong International	New York	Darryl Adachi	www.armstrongint.com
Bialecki	New York	Linda Bialecki	www.bialecki.com
Choi & Burns	New York	Julie Choi	www.choiburns.com
Cromwell Partners	New York	Joseph Ziccardi	www.cromwell-partners.com
DDJ Myers	Phoenix	Dee Dee Myers	www.ddjmyers.com
Dowd Associates	White Plains	Richard Dowd	www.dowdassociates.com
Fiderion Financial Services Group	Atlanta	James Norton	www.fiderion.com
Higdon Associates	New York	Henry Higdon	www.higdonbarret.com
Gilbert Tweed	New York	Janet Tweed	www.gilberttweed.com
Jay Gaines & Co	New York	Jay Gaines & Co	www.jaygaines.com
Michael Page	New York	Dean Ball	www.michaelpage.com
The Ogdon Partnership	New York	Thomas H. Ogdon	www.ogdon.com
Prince Goldsmith	New York	Marylin Prince	www.princegoldsmith.com
Quorum	New York	Chuck Barrett	www.quorumsearch.com
Rhodes Associates	New York	Scott Coff	www.rhodesassociates.com
Ropes Associates	Fort Lauderdale	John Ropes	www.ropesassociates.com
Sextant Search	New York	Steven B. Potter	www.sextant.com
Whitney Group	New York	Gary Goldstein	www.whitneygroup.com

Asia

Alexander Mann	Hong Kong	Mike Brennan	www.alexmann.com
Eban International	Hong Kong	Stephen McAlinden	www.eban.com
Executive Access	Hong Kong	Max Loomis	www.execaccess.com
Global Sage	Hong Kong	May Koon	www.globalsage.com
Henderson Baillieu	Hong Kong	Nick Henderson	n/a
Hogarth Davies Lloyd	Hong Kong	Guy Davies	www.hogarthdavieslloyd.com
		James Hogarth	

Pelham Search Pacific	Hong Kong Mark Jones	www.pelhaminternational. com
Robertson Smart	Hong Kong Gareth Stubblings	www.robertsonsmart. com
Whitney Group	Hong Kong Harry O'Neill	www.whitneygroup.com

Global firms' practice leaders

Company	Location	Consultant
Amrop Hever	Zurich	Fredy Hausammann
A.T. Kearney	New York	Kenneth Rich
Boyden	New York	Jeanne Branthover
Christian & Timbers	Stamford	Mark A. Esposito
Egon Zehnder	London; Munich	Andrew Lowenthal; Stefan Reckhenrich
Eric Salmon	Milan; Paris	Hans Phoenes; Sophie Wigniolle
Globe Search	London	Ian Lazarus
Heidrick & Struggles	New York	Michael Franzino
Highland Partners	New York; Chicago	Gerard G. Cameron; Michael J. Corey
IIC Partners	London	David Timson
Korn/Ferry	London	L. Parker Harrell Jr
Ray & Berndtson	Brussels; Frankfurt	Alain De Borchgrave (insurance); Christine Kuhl (asset management, private banking)
Russell Reynolds	London; New York; Singapore	Simon Hearn; John Rogan; Choon Soo Chew
Spencer Stuart	London	Jason Chaffer
Stanton Chase	Madrid	Jorge Fidalgo Urgoiti
Transearch	Paris; Chicago	Carlos Gravato; Audrey Hellinger
Whitehead Mann	London	Chris Leslie

Media, entertainment, publishing, sports management

This sector includes the entertainment fields of television, broadcasting, publishing, media, new media, software (also covered by the technology sector), advertising, PR and communications, as well as the new sector of sports management. This category is particularly suited to small boutiques and many of the specialists are based in important media centres such as New York, Los Angeles, London and Hong Kong.

Boutiques

Company	Location	Consultant	Website
Bird & Co	London	Isabel Bird	www.bird-co.com
Bó Lè	Hong Kong	Louisa Rousseau	www.bo-le.com
Exeller	Madrid	Jorge Boixeda	www.exeller.com
R. Gatti & Associates	New York	Robert Gatti	www.gattihr.com
Gould McCoy Chadick & Ellig	New York	Millicent McCoy	www.gmcsearch.com
Herbert Mines	New York	Harold Reiter	www.herbertmines.com
HVS Executive Search	New York	Keith Kefgen	www.hvsinternational.com
Jay Gaines & Co	New York	Jay Gaines	www.jaygaines.com
Miles Partnership	London	Miles Broadbent	www.globesearchgroup.com
Moyer Sherwood Associates	New York	David Moyer	www.moyersherwood.com
WTW Executive Search	New York	Warren Wasp	www.wtwassociates.com

Global firms' practice leaders

Company	Location	Consultant
Amrop Hever	London	Stephen Bampfylde
Christian & Timbers	New York	Paula Seibel
Eric Salmon	London; Paris	Aileen Taylor; Christian Lanis
Heidrick & Struggles	Tysons Corner	Michael J. Flagg
Korn/Ferry	Los Angeles	Bill Simon
Spencer Stuart	Los Angeles; London	Judy Havas; Jan Hall

Non-executive directors and boards

This category includes CEOs and board members. Because of the increased emphasis on good corporate governance following corporate scandals such as Enron in the early 2000s, the recruitment of CEOs, non-executive directors and board members is growing. Most of the global firms have a practice dedicated to work in this sector, and Spencer Stuart and Heidrick & Struggles are considered to be the dominant players. There are also a growing number of well-respected boutique firms which are dedicated to working at this level only. Many of the specialists are based in the United States (New York) and the UK (London), but the market for non-executive and board directors is also growing in Germany and other European countries.

Boutiques

Company	Location	Consultant	Website
33 St James's	London	Bruce Beringer	www.33stjamess.com
Atkinson Stuart	Zug (Switzerland)	Rudolf Schicker	www.atkinsonstuart.com
Boardroom Consultants	New York	Roger Kenney	www.boardrooomconsultants.com
Cordiner King Hever	Melbourne	Richard King	www.amrophever.com
Garner International	London	Andrew Garner	www.garnerintl.com
Groupe Mercator	Paris	François Carn	www.groupemercator.com
Jones & Partner	London	Ian Jones	www.ianjonesandpartners.com
Zygos	London	Julia Budd John Viney	www.zygos.com

Global firms' practice leaders

Company	Location	Consultant
Amrop Hever	Johannesburg	Sandra Burmeister
A.T. Kearney	Fort Worth	Paul Ray Jr
Boyden	San Francisco	Fred Greene
Egon Zehnder	Paris	Christopher W. Thomas
Eric Salmon	Paris	Eric Salmon
Globe Search	London; New York	Miles Broadbent & Nigel Smith; Harold Reiter
Heidrick & Struggles	New York	Joie A. Gregor
Highland Partners	Los Angeles	Robert Rollo
Korn/Ferry	London; Paris; New York	Mina Gouran; Didier Vuchot; Charles H. King
Russell Reynolds	Chicago	Charles Tribbett; Andrea Redmond
Spencer Stuart	London; Paris	David Kimbell; Henri de Pitray
Stanton Chase	New York	Andrew Sherwood
Transearch	Paris	Alain Tanugi
Whitehead Mann	London	Carol Leonard

Not-for-profit, foundations, public sector

This sector is more established in the United States than elsewhere but it is growing worldwide. It includes search for executives in educational institutions, non-profit foundations, charities, cultural associations (such as museums) and governments. Increasingly, it also includes a new sub-division, diversity, which assists clients in addressing the issues of gender, ethnic and racial diversity in hiring. There are a number of established not-for-profit boutiques in the United States.

In Europe, Odgers Ray & Berndtson, Saxton Bampfylde, Whitehead Mann and Heidrick & Struggles are well known for not-for-profit and public-sector work, especially consultants Virginia Bottomley at Odgers Ray & Berndtson and Gill Lewis at Heidrick & Struggles, both of whom are based in London.

Boutiques

Company	Location	Consultant	Website
Bridgestar	Boston	Kathleen Yazbak-Chartier	www.bridgestar.org
Brigham Hill Consultancy	Dallas	Lincoln Eldredge	www.brighamhill.com

Global firms' practice leaders

Company	Location	Consultant
A.T. Kearney	Alexandria	Shelly Storbeck
Heidrick & Struggles	London; New York	Gill Lewis; Nathaniel J. Sutton
Korn/Ferry	Washington DC (not-for-profit, government); Dallas (education)	Charles Ingersoll (not-for-profit, government); Bill Funk (education)
Ray & Berndtson	London	Frances Bell, Virginia Bottomley
Russell Reynolds	Washington DC	Eric Vautour (associations, government affairs); Malcolm MacKay, Mary Tydings (not-for-profit)
Spencer Stuart	Washington DC	Mike Kirkman

Pharmaceuticals, life sciences, biotechnology

Leaders in the rapidly expanding heath-care and life sciences sector must have a deep understanding of both the science and business of health care. Some search consultants have medical degrees, some have a background in research and others have been industry analysts. Sub-categories include life sciences, biotechnology (a fast-growing area), medical devices and diagnostics, health-care technology and outsourcing, managed care and consumer pharmaceuticals. Most of the larger firms have global practice groups, notably Korn/Ferry, Spencer Stuart, Russell Reynolds and Highland Partners. There are also boutiques throughout the United States and in the UK (London), and they are starting to develop elsewhere in Europe. Health-care clients can range from early-stage, venture-capital-backed companies to fully integrated global manufacturers, hospitals, health-care technology companies, managed care and health-care consulting firms.

Boutiques

Company	Location	Consultant	Website
Ballein Search Partners	Oakbrook	Kathleen Ballein	n/a
Day and Associates	San Francisco	J. Kevin Day	www.dayassociates.net
The Domann Organization	Rancho Santa Fe	William Domann	www.domann.net
Diversified Search	Philadelphia	Judith van Seldeneck	www.divsearch.com
Euromedica	London	Peter Woods	www.euromedica.com
Exeller	Madrid	Jorge Boixeda	www.exeller.com
Highland Partners	Encino	Neal Maslan	www.highlandsearch.com
Reeder & Associates	Roswell	Michael Redder	www.reederassoc.com
Ruston Poole	London	David Collingham	www.rustonpoole.com
Tyler & Company	Atlanta	Larry Tyler	www.tylerandco.com
Witt/Kieffer	Oakbrook	Jordan Hadelman	www.wittkieffer.com

Global firms' practice leaders

Company	Location	Consultant
Amrop Hever	Copenhagen	Eskil Westh
A.T. Kearney	Chicago	Henry J. Scherck
Boyden	London	Lisa Gerhard
Egon Zehnder	Chicago	Louis Kacyn
Eric Salmon	Frankfurt; Paris	Claudia Schuetz; Laurence Vienot
Globe Search	London	Simon Bartholomew
Heidrick & Struggles	Los Angeles; Sydney; Copenhagen	Richard N. Eidinger; Filomena Leonardi; Tobias Petri
Highland Partners	London; Encino	Fallya Petrakopoulou; Neal Maslan
IIC Partners	Milan	Luca Temellini
Korn/Ferry	Princeton	Cheryl Buxton

Ray & Berndtson	Amsterdam	Michael Mellink
Russell Reynolds	Dallas; Amsterdam	Jay Kizer; Jacques Bouwens
Spencer Stuart	New York	Joseph Bocuzzi
Stanton Chase	Austin	David Harap
Transearch	Amsterdam	Michel de Boer
Whitehead Mann	London	Chris Burrows

Professional services

This sector includes accounting, tax, human resources, legal and consulting firms as well as senior level functional positions within these categories (such as chief financial officer, chief information officer). Legal and HR specialists are often part of this practice group too. Consulting is sometimes part of the technology or financial services practice groups at headhunting firms that do not have a dedicated professional services group.

Boutiques

Company	Location	Consultant	Website
33 St James's	London	Bruce Beringer	www.33stjamess.com
Bao & Partners	Madrid	Richard Taunton	www.baopartners.com
The Executive Source	New York	Sarah Marks	www.executivesource.com
Gatti & Associates	Boston	Robert D Gatti	www.gattihr.com
Gould McCoy Chadick & Ellig	New York	Susan Chadick	www.gmcsearch.com
Patricia Wilson Associates	San Francisco	Patricia Wilson	www.penhryn.com

Global firms' practice leaders

Company	Location	Consultant
A.T. Kearney	London; Atlanta	Beth Knight; Stephen Dezember
Christian & Timbers	New York	Adam Prager
Egon Zehnder	London	Ashley Summerfeld
Eric Salmon	London	Anthony Harling
Heidrick & Struggles	Tysons Corner	J. Eric Joseph, Krishnan Rajagopalan
Highland Partners	Stamford; San Francisco	Darren G. Romano (HR); Kristin Hebert (legal)
Korn/Ferry	Dallas (HR); New York & Stamford (legal)	Gregory Hessel (HR); Julie Goldberg & Keith Wimbush (legal)
Ray & Berndtson	Frankfurt	Michael Proft

Russell Reynolds	Belgium	Jean van den Eynde (legal)
Spencer Stuart	London	Caroline Eadie; Simon Russell
Stanton Chase	Los Angeles	Ed Savage
Whitehead Mann	London	Anthony May

Technology and telecoms

This sector includes communications and convergence, software and services, hardware and electronics. Given the fast-paced nature of the sector, there is much change and innovation. The global firms are well represented, especially Heidrick & Struggles, Korn/Ferry, Egon Zehnder, Christian & Timbers and ITP. Many boutiques also operate in this sector, especially in technology centres such as Silicon Valley.

Boutiques

Company	Location	Consultant	Website
Bishop Partners	New York	Susan Bishop	www.bishoppartners.com
Harvey Nash	London	Nick Marsh	www.harveynash.com
Hoggett Bowers	London	John Carter	www.hoggett-bowers.com
Herbert Mines	New York	Hal Reiter	www.herbertmines.com
Jay Gaines	New York	Jay Gaines	www.jaygaines.com
Jouve & Associés	Paris	Michel Flasaquier, Josette Sayers	www.jouve-associes.com
Marlar Bennetts International	London	Robin Marlar	www.marlar.com
Mercier & Partners	Paris	Thierry Mercier	www.mercier-partners.com
Rusher Loscavio & Lopresto	San Francisco	William Rusher	www.rll.com
SES Asia	Singapore	Hsiao Yuan Li	www.sesasia.com
Skott/Edwards	Morristown	Skott Burkland	www.skottedwards.com
Traub & Associates	Taipei	Christopher Traub	n/a

Global firms' practice leaders

Company	Location	Consultant
Amrop Hever	Vienna; San Mateo	Andreas Landgrebe; John Ferneborg
A.T. Kearney	New York	Lisa Hooker
Boyden	San Francisco	Bob Concannon

Christian & Timbers	London; Cleveland	Piers Marmion; Brian Sullivan
Egon Zehnder	Atlanta, Palo Alto, San Francisco	S. Ross Brown
Eric Salmon	London; Paris	Anthony Harling; Didier Duval
Globe Search	London	Nigel Backwith
Heidrick & Struggles	Munich; Cleveland; Menlo Park	Mathias Hiebeler (consumer technology, entertainment); Michael Nieset (hardware, systems, software); Tim O'Shea (semiconductors)
Highland Partners	Dallas	James M. Bethmann
IIC Partners	Washington DC	Paul Dinte
ITP Worldwide	Boston; Houston; Larkspur	Charles Polachi; R. Paul Kors; Lee Schweichler
Korn/Ferry	Los Angeles	Richard Spitz
Penrhyn	London; Brussels; Zurich	Christopher Mill; Anders Borg; Roy Hitchman
Ray & Berndtson	Frankfurt	Michael Proft
Russell Reynolds	London	Kai Hammerich
Spencer Stuart	San Mateo	James Buckley
Stanton Chase	Zurich	Lucas Schellenberg
Transearch	Paris	Alain Roca
Whitehead Mann	London	Graham Jones

Appendix 1 **Glossary**

Assignment	Commission from a client to a headhunter to carry out a search for a specific position
Associate	A junior consultant within a search firm, ranking below consultant and partner
Beauty parade	When several search firms compete for the same client (a competitive pitch)
Benchbuilding	After a succession planning process gaps may be exposed in the management team where there is no obvious person ready to move into them if the incumbents should leave or be promoted. Once the gaps have been identified, it is necessary to "build the bench" of successors under each one through either promotion or recruiting
Benchmark candidate	Evaluate according to set criteria, often using examples known to client and consultant
Billings	Fee income including expenses of search firms; billings may include fees from searches generated as well as searches executed. Firms add up billings differently
Blackball	To downgrade, denigrate or flag candidates so that they are not considered or considered only with caution for any assignment
Boutique firm	Small firm typically specialising in one sector, function or region
Brief profile	Detailed document which acts as a control on the search and outlines the expected time plan and headhunter fees
Cap	Ceiling on fees regardless of compensation level; for example, a company may insist on a $50,000 cap on fees even if the headhunter normally charges a fee of 33% of a candidate's compensation
Completion	Usually when candidates start work, sometimes when they sign a contract of employment and sometimes when they resign from their current job
Consultant	A general term loosely applied to all headhunters, as opposed to researchers
Contingency-based recruitment	When the search firm's pay is contingent upon the success of the assignment
Courtesy interview	When a candidate is interviewed because a friend of the

	search firm (or client) asked that it be done, even if the candidate is not appropriate for any of the active searches
CV/résumé – chronological and functional	Chronological is historical, based on time, showing education and work experience; functional cites key traits, experience by function (cost-cutter, inspirational leader)
Emotional intelligence	Emotional traits that are increasingly important in the evaluation of a candidate; for example, self-awareness, persistence, motivation, empathy
Executive coaching	A service offered by search firms where an individual or team is offered expert advice on how to enhance performance
Expenses	Expenses or costs related to the search incurred by a search firm. These generally include out-of-pocket expenses such as travel and meals, and allocated expenses such as mailing, secretarial, report production and communications. Such expenses often add 8–12% to the cost of the retainer
Fee income	Income a search firm receives from fees charged to the client excluding expenses
Flagged individual	Candidate with known problems or issues; for example, the individual cannot relocate or poor references were received
Functional practice group	Headhunters organise their teams into industry and functional practice groups. Examples of functional groups are chief financial officers (CFOs), chief information officers (CIOs), legal, marketing, HR
Golden handcuffs	An incentive, usually financial, applied by a company to executives as an inducement to stay and not be tempted by headhunters to move. Such incentives can include pensions, equity which vests over a period of time, loans and other benefits
Guarantee	Many search firms offer clients a guarantee that they will continue to search if the assignment is not completed in a specific period of time or if a successful candidate leaves within six months
Industry practice group	Headhunters organise their teams into industry or sector specialists known as practice groups. Examples include automotive, consumer, energy, financial services, media, life sciences
Initial brief	Proposal letter from the search firm to the client firm, outlining their understanding of the assignment
Job hopper	Candidate who switches jobs frequently, often staying at a company for less than three years

Key account manager	A search firm's relationship manager for a specific client company; for example, key account manager for the Coca-Cola Company
Long list	Initial list of all possible candidates for an assignment, usually compiled by research before candidates are approached by the headhunter
Management assessment	A service offered by search firms to assess both individuals and teams (including boards) for specific roles
New boy network	A system of personal contacts, based on professional firms or business schools; for example, Goldman Sachs, McKinsey, Harvard
Non-compete clause	An agreement to prevent headhunters at large firms leaving to set up in direct competition. The non-compete clause usually lasts between 12 and 24 months
Off-limits	Companies that are current or recent clients of a search firm and may not be approached in the search for candidates. Such companies are seen as poaching grounds
Old boy network	A system of personal contacts based on schools, universities, social clubs or sports clubs
Outsourced research	When a search firm asks an outside party to conduct its research on a particular candidate or market
Parallel processing	When a candidate is considered for two assignments at the same time
Placement	Successful assignment completed by the search firm
Practice group	A specialist group within a search firm that focuses on a specific sector of the market; for example, automotive, consumer, financial services, life sciences, telecoms
Preferred supplier	When clients designate specific search firms as the only ones they will use
Reference checks	When the search consultant asks individuals who know or have worked with the candidate for a reference
Referrals	When a client recommends a search firm to another or when a candidate is called and suggests several potential individuals for an assignment
Researcher	A member of the staff of a headhunting firm who undertakes research work as opposed to being a consultant. There are many levels of researcher including research associate, research consultant and research manager. Generally they have no direct contact with candidates but identify them through database research or cold calls to target companies

Retainer	A search firm is employed by a client for a fee (the retainer) whether the search is completed or not. The retainer may be a fixed amount or a percentage of a candidate's annual salary. It is usually paid over a three-month period
Revenue	The total income of a search firm, including expenses on top of fee income
Revolving retainer	Perpetual renewal of a retainer
Screening	The process of sorting through a large number of preliminary candidates in order to arrive at a shortlist
Shoot out	When several search firms compete for the same client (a competitive pitch)
Shortlist	The final list of candidates presented by the consultant to the client, typically three or four possible contenders, all of whom have expressed real interest in the position
Source	A person contacted to suggest a possible candidate for an assignment
Specialist firm	A search firm that specialises in recruiting in one or a few particular sectors, by industry or function
Stick rate	How long a candidate has stayed in his or her placement. This is generally measured as the percentage of placements that remain with a company for at least 2–3 years
Success rate	The proportion of assignments successfully completed by a search firm as opposed to those that had to be abandoned or were cancelled by the client. On average 70–80% of assignments are completed successfully
Transaction-based firm	A search firm that seeks to maximise its volume of business in terms of number of assignments. Such firms do not necessarily enjoy a large percentage of repeat business because they develop little or no relationship with the client, who sees them as commodity providers rather than long-term partners
Write in	CVs sent by hopeful would-be candidates to the firm in contrast to personally referred candidates or those targeted through research
White knight	A particularly able business executive, usually recommended by a headhunter, brought in by a company to help fight off an unwelcome takeover bid from a competitor or other outsider
Wild card	A candidate that does not meet the job specification requirements but is still included in the shortlist for another reason

Appendix 2
Association of Executive Search Consultants: list of worldwide members

The Association of Executive Search Consultants (AESC) is the worldwide professional organisation for retained executive search consulting firms (for further information see pages 23–26).

North America
12 East 41st Street
New York, NY 10017
US
Tel: +1 212 398 9556

Europe
Rue Washington 40, Box 20
1050 Brussels
Belgium
Tel: +32 2 733 36 31
Website: www.aesc.org

Europe
Austria
Ecker & Partner/Signium International
Heidrick & Struggles
Jenewein & Partner/The Amrop Hever
  Group
Korn/Ferry International
Neumann International
Ray & Berndtson
Spencer Stuart
Transearch International

Belgium
A.T. Kearney Executive Search
Amrop International/The Amrop Hever
  Group
Boyden
Euromedica Group
Hansar International/Penrhyn
  International
Heidrick & Struggles
Korn/Ferry International
Neumann International
Ray & Berndtson
Russell Reynolds Associates

Spencer Stuart
The Hever Group/The Amrop Hever
  Group
Transearch International

Bulgaria
Stein & Partner Management
  Consulting/The Amrop Hever
  Group
Neumann International

Croatia
Neumann International

Czech Republic
Accord ECE
Boyden
Dr Kaufmann & Partner/The Amrop
  Hever Group
Neumann International
Ray & Berndtson
Spencer Stuart

Denmark
Amrop Hever AS/The Amrop Hever
   Group
Boyden
Causa Consulting/Signium
   International
Euromedica Group
Heidrick & Struggles
Korn/Ferry International
Ray & Berndtson
Russell Reynolds Associates
Transearch International

Estonia
Executive Search Baltics/The Amrop
   Hever Group

Finland
Boyden
Amrop Hever Finland/The Amrop
   Hever Group
Heidrick & Struggles
Korn/Ferry International
Ray & Berndtson
Scandinavian Search &
   Selection/Signium
International
Transearch International

France
A.T. Kearney Executive Search
Boyden
Euromedica Group
Groupe Mercator
Heidrick & Struggles
Korn/Ferry International
Lang, Boyer et Associés/Penrhyn
   International
Leaders Trust International
Mercier & Partners
Meridian
Mindoor Executive Search
Neumann International
Ray & Berndtson
Russell Reynolds Associates
Acteurop/The Amrop Hever Group
Hommes & Enterprises/The Amrop
   Hever Group

Rossignol Tod & Associés/The Amrop
   Hever Group
Eric Salmon & Partners
Singer & Hamilton
Spencer Stuart
Transearch International

Germany
A.T. Kearney Executive Search
Boyden
Eric Salmon & Partners
Euromedica Group
Heidrick & Struggles
Korn/Ferry International
Mindoor Executive Search
Nedelcu & Company/Leading Edge
   Executives
Neumann International
Lachner Aden Beyer & Company
   GmbH/Penrhyn International
Ray & Berndtson
Russell Reynolds Associates
Signium International
Spencer Stuart
DELTA Management Consultants
   GmbH/The Amrop Hever Group
Transearch International

Greece
Boyden
HR Exsel Ltd/The Amrop Hever Group
Korn/Ferry International

Hungary
Accord ECE
Boyden
Kohlmann & Young Management
   Consulting/The Amrop Hever
   Group
Korn/Ferry International
Neumann International
Ray & Berndtson
Spencer Stuart
Transearch International

Ireland
Amrop Hever Ireland/The Amrop
   Hever Group

McEvoy Associates/Signium
   International
MERC Partners
Transearch International

Italy
A.T. Kearney Executive Search
Boyden
D & G/The Amrop Hever Group
Eric Salmon & Partners
Heidrick & Struggles
Korn/Ferry International
Leaders Trust International
Mindoor Executive Search
Neumann International
Neusearch/Signium International
Ray & Berndtson
Russell Reynolds Associates
Spencer Stuart
Transearch International

Latvia
Executive Search Baltics SIA/The
   Amrop Hever Group

Luxembourg
Korn/Ferry International

Netherlands
A.T. Kearney Executive Search
Amrop International/The Amrop Hever
   Group
BJW Executive Search/Signium
   International
Boyden
Heidrick & Struggles
Korn/Ferry International
Leaders-Trust International
Mindoor Executive Search
Ray & Berndtson
Russell Reynolds Associates
Spencer Stuart
Transearch International

Norway
A.T. Kearney Executive Search
Amrop International/The Amrop Hever
   Group
Boyden

Korn/Ferry International
Ray & Berndtson
Russell Reynolds Associates
Transearch International

Poland
Accord ECE
Boyden
Dr Prasuhn & Partner/Signium
   International
Gow & Partners
Heidrick & Struggles
Korn/Ferry International
LAN Partners/The Amrop Hever Group
Neumann International
Ray & Berndtson
Russell Reynolds Associates
Spencer Stuart
RSQ Management/Transearch

Portugal
Amrop International/The Amrop Hever
   Group
Boyden
Heidrick & Struggles
Ray & Berndtson
Transearch International

Romania
Accord ECE
Leadership Development Solutions
Stein & Partner Management
   Consulting/The Amrop Hever
   Group

Russia
Boyden
KBS Associates Ltd/The Amrop Hever
   Group
Korn/Ferry International
Neumann International
Ray & Berndtson
RosExpert

Serbia
Neumann International

Slovak Republic
Accord ECE

Jenewein & Partners/The Amrop Hever Group

Slovenia
Neumann International

Spain
A.T. Kearney Executive Search
Bao & Partners
Boyden
EuroGalenus/Penrhyn International
Exeller
Heidrick & Struggles
Korn/Ferry International
Leaders-Trust International
Mindoor Executive Search
Neumann International
Norman Broadbent/Transearch
Ray & Berndtson
Referal Partners International/The Amrop Hever Group
Russell Reynolds Associates
Seeliger y Conde/The Amrop Hever Group
Spencer Stuart
Transearch International
Zavala Gortari Asociados

Sweden
Amrop International/The Amrop Hever Group
Boyden
Delectus Hever AB/The Amrop Hever Group
Hansar International/Penrhyn International
Heidrick & Struggles
A.T. Kearney Executive Search
Korn/Ferry International
Mindoor Executive Search
Ray & Berndtson
Russell Reynolds Associates
SIMS/Signium International
Spencer Stuart
Transearch International

Switzerland
A.T. Kearney Executive Search
Atkinson Stuart

Boyden
Dr Besmer Consulting/The Amrop Hever Group
Engels & Harzheim/Signium International
Heidrick & Struggles
Korn/Ferry International
Leaders-Trust International
Orbis Executive Search/Transearch
Ray & Berndtson
Roy C. Hitchman AG/Penrhyn International
SPECTRAsearch AG/The Amrop Hever Group
Spencer Stuart
Transearch Dayak/Transearch

Turkey
Amrop Hever Turkey/The Amrop Hever Group
Boyden
Heidrick & Struggles
K Partners International
Neumann International
Ray & Berndtson

UK
A.T. Kearney Executive Search
Boyden
Christopher Mill & Partners/Penrhyn International
Eric Salmon & Partners
Euromedica Group
Garner International
Glenn Irvine International
Gow & Partners
Gundersen Bucher Rugman
Heidrick & Struggles
Korn/Ferry International
MERC Partners
Mindoor Executive Search
Moloney Search
Norman Broadbent/Transearch
Osprey Clarke/Penrhyn International
Odgers/Ray & Berndtson
Russell Reynolds Associates
Saxton Bampfylde Hever/The Amrop Hever Group
Singer & Hamilton

Spencer Stuart
Whitney Group

North America
Canada
A.T. Kearney Executive Search
BDK Global Search
Boyden
Enns Partners/The Amrop Hever Group
Heidrick & Struggles
Janet Wright & Associates
Knightsbridge Executive Search
Korn/Ferry International
Legacy Executive Search Partners
Michel Pauzé & Associés/Transearch
Ray & Berndtson
Russell Reynolds Associates
Spencer Stuart
The Bedford Consulting
    Group/Transearch International
    Partners
The Caldwell Partners
The Executive Source
The Verriez Group

United States
A.T. Kearney Executive Search
Alexander Associates
Allen Austin Executive
    Search/Transearch
Anderson & Associates
Anthony Michael & Company
Avery James
Baker Parker Associates/The Amrop
    Hever Group
Ballein Search Partners
Battalia Winston International
Bialecki
Boardroom Consultants
Bonell Ryan
Boyden
Bridgestar
Brigham Hill Consultancy
Capstone Partnership
CareerSmith
Carrington & Carrington
Clarence E. McFeely

Clarey Andrews & Klein/Penrhyn
    International
Coleman Lew & Associates
Columbia Consulting Group
Compass Group/The Amrop Hever
    Group
Curran Partners/Eurosearch
    Consultants
D.P. Parker and Associates
Day & Associates
Deborah Snow Walsh
Dennis P. O'Toole & Associates
Dieckmann & Associates
Dowd Associates
EFL Associates/Transearch
Epsen, Fuller & Associates
Eric Salmon & Partners
Ferneborg & Associates
Fiderion Financial Services Group
Francis & Associates
Gardiner International
Gould, McCoy, Chadick & Ellig
Gow & Partners
Grisham Group LLC
Gundersen Bucher Rugman
Halbrecht Lieberman Associates
Heidrick & Struggles
Globe Search Group/Herbert Mines
    Associates
Herrerias & Associates
Higdon Barrett
HRD Consultants
Hunt Howe Partners
J.B. Homer Associates
Jay Gaines & Company
Kincannon & Reed
Kinser & Baillou
Korn/Ferry International
Martin H. Bauman Associates
Martin Partners
McBride Associates
Meridian Partners/Signium
    International
Michael Kelly Associates
Moyer, Sherwood Associates
Nordeman Grimm
Norman Broadbent/Transearch
Preng & Associates

Raines International
Ray & Berndtson
Reeder & Associates
Rhodes Associates
Robert W. Dingman Company
Ropes Associates
Rurak & Associates
Rusher, Loscavio & LoPresto
Russell Reynolds Associates
SeBA International
Seeliger y Conde International –
    Miami/The Amrop Hever Group
Signium International
Skott Edwards Consultants/Penrhyn
    International
Smith and Syberg
Sockwell & Associates/Transearch
Spence Associates International
Spencer Stuart
Sunny Bates Associates
Synergistics Associates
Thacher Executive Search
The Directorship Search Group
The Diversified Search Companies
The Domann Organization
The Holman Group
The John Lucht Consultancy
The McIntyre Company
The Onstott Group/World Search
    Group
The Prout Group
Virchaux & Partners
Whitehead Mann Pendleton James
Whitney Group
William Willis Worldwide/World
    Search Group
WTW Associates/IIC Partner
Wyatt & Jaffe

Latin America
Argentina
Boyden
Heidrick & Struggles
Korn/Ferry International
Ray & Berndtson
Russell Reynolds Associates
Seeliger y Conde Argentina/The Amrop
    Hever Group

Spencer Stuart
Voyer International/Penrhyn
    International

Brazil
A.T. Kearney Executive Search
Boyden
Dobroy & Partners International
FESA Global Recruiters/IIC Partner
Heidrick & Struggles
Korn/Ferry International
Leaders-Trust International
Panelli Motta Cabrera &
    Associados/The Amrop Hever
    Group
Ray & Berndtson
Russell Reynolds Associates
Signium International
Spencer Stuart
Transearch International

Chile
Boyden
Heidrick & Struggles
Korn/Ferry International
MV Amrop/The Amrop Hever Group
Ray & Berndtson
Spencer Stuart
Transearch International

Colombia
Boyden
Heidrick & Struggles
Korn/Ferry International
Spencer Stuart
Top Management/The Amrop Hever
    Group

Ecuador
Amrop Hever – Ecuador/The Amrop
    Hever Group
Korn/Ferry International

Mexico
Boyden
Echelon SA de CV/The Amrop Hever
    Group
Heidrick & Struggles

Korn/Ferry International
Ray & Berndtson
Seeliger y Conde Internacional SA de
    CV/The Amrop Hever Group
Russell Reynolds Associates
SH-Search
Spencer Stuart
Transearch International Partners

Peru
Boyden
Amrop Hever Peru/The Amrop Hever
    Group
Heidrick & Struggles
Korn/Ferry International
Transearch International/Transearch
    Lima

Venezuela
Boyden
Conteven CA
Crease Consultores/The Amrop Hever
    Group
Heidrick & Struggles
Korn/Ferry International
Transearch International Partners

Asia and Australasia
Australia
A.T. Kearney Executive Search
Boyden
Cordiner King/The Amrop Hever Group
Fish & Nankivell Ogilvie
    Watson/Penrhyn International
Heidrick & Struggles
Korn/Ferry International
NORS Partners
Ray & Berndtson
Russell Reynolds Associates
Spencer Stuart
The Asia Partnership
The Insight Group
Watermark Search
    International/Transearch

China
Amrop Hever China/The Amrop Hever
    Group

Heidrick & Struggles
Korn/Ferry International
Ray & Berndtson
Russell Reynolds Associates
Spencer Stuart

Hong Kong
Amrop Hever China/The Amrop Hever
    Group
A.T. Kearney Executive Search
Bennett Associates Limited
Boyden
Gow & Partners
Heidrick & Struggles
Korn/Ferry International
Ray & Berndtson
Russell Reynolds Associates
Spencer Stuart
The Asia Partnerhship
Wright Company/Transearch
Whitney Group

India
3P Consultants Pvt/Penrhyn
    International
Amrop International/The Amrop Hever
    Group
Boyden
Heidrick & Struggles
Korn/Ferry International
Ray & Berndtson
Transearch International

Indonesia
Amrop Hever Indonesia/The Amrop
    Hever Group
Boyden
Korn/Ferry International

Japan
A.T. Kearney Executive Search
Boyden
Heidrick & Struggles
Jomon Associates/The Amrop Hever
    Group
Korn/Ferry International
Ray & Berndtson
Russell Reynolds Associates

Shimamoto Partners/Penrhyn
   Interntional
Signium International
Spencer Stuart
The Asia Partnership
Transearch International

Korea
Amrop Hever Korea/The Amrop Hever
   Group
Boyden
Heidrick & Struggles
Korn/Ferry International
Search International
Top Business Consultant
   Services/Signium International
Unico Search/Transearch

Malaysia
Bennett Associates
Boyden
Garner International
Korn/Ferry Interntional
Signium World Executive
   Search/Signium International
Transearch International

New Zealand
Bell McCaw Bampfylde/The Amrop
   Hever Group
Boyden
Executive Search International/Signium
   International
John Peebles Associates World Search
   Group
Korn/Ferry International

Philippines
Boyden
Signium International
The Executive Edge/The Amrop Hever
   Group

Singapore
A.T. Kearney Executive Search
Gattie-Tan Soo Jin Management
   Consultants/The Amrop Hever
   Group

Boyden
Heidrick & Struggles
Korn/Ferry International
PHR Group Asia Pacific
Ray & Berndtson
Russell Reynolds Associates
Spencer Stuart

Taiwan
BoydenTaipei
Dynatech Business Associates/The
   Amrop Hever Group
Heidrick & Struggles

Thailand
Advantage Executive Recruitment/The
   Amrop Hever Group
Boyden
Korn/Ferry International
Wright Company/Transearch

Middle East and Africa
Kuwait
Transearch International

Lebanon
The Amrop Hever Group/The Amrop
   Hever Group – RASD

Saudi Arabia
The Amrop Hever Group/The Amrop
   Hever Group – RASD

South Africa
Boyden
Heidrick & Struggles
Korn/Ferry International
Landelahni Amrop Hever/The Amrop
   Hever Group
Ray & Berndtson
Spencer Stuart
Transearch International

United Arab Emirates
Korn/Ferry International
RASD Ltd/The Amrop Hever Group
Ray & Berndtson

Appendix 3 Useful addresses

Executive Grapevine International Ltd
New Barnes Mill
Cottonmill Lane
St Albans AL1 2HA
UK
Tel: +44 1727 844335
E-mail: enquiries@executive-grapevine.co.uk
Website: www.askgrapevine.com
A research and publishing firm which tracks the executive recruitment and human capital markets. It publishes directories of executive recruiters and a magazine, *The Grapevine Magazine*.

Executive Search Information Services (ESIS)
124 Willard Hill Road
Harrisville, NH 03450
US
Tel: +1 603 563 3456
E-mail: david@davidlord.com

Hunt-Scanlon Corporation
700 Fairfield Avenue
Stamford, CT 06902
US
Tel: +1 203 352 2920
Website: www.hunt-scanlon.com
A research and publishing firm in executive recruiting and human capital. It publishes newsletters, *Executive Search Review*, *Online Recruiting Strategist* and *Diversity Monitor*, and directories of executive recruiters.

Kennedy Information Inc
One Phoenix Mill Lane, 5th floor
Peterborough, NH 03458
US
Tel: +1 603 924 1006
Website: www.kennedyinfo.com
A publishing and research company which covers executive recruiting

and other professional services. It publishes newsletters, *Executive Recruiter News* and *Recruiting Trends*, and an annual *Directory of Executive Recruiters*.

Intercultural Business Improvement
Eemnesserweg 11-05
1251 NA Laren
Netherlands
Tel: +31 35 629 4269
Website: www.ibinet.nl
A research and publishing company which has developed the Intercultural Readiness Check. This uses four competencies:

- Intercultural sensitivity – flexibility in taking different perspectives and interest in cultural norms and values.
- Intercultural communication – flexibility in communication across cultures.
- Building commitment – the ability to stimulate co-operation between people and to take the lead while at the same time keeping others on board.
- Managing uncertainty – the ability to manage the greater uncertainty of intercultural situations.